AF478294

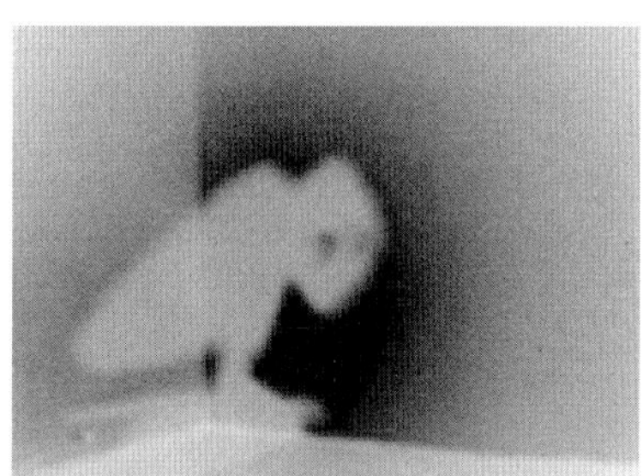

Sleepless

Nights

OLIVER HERRING

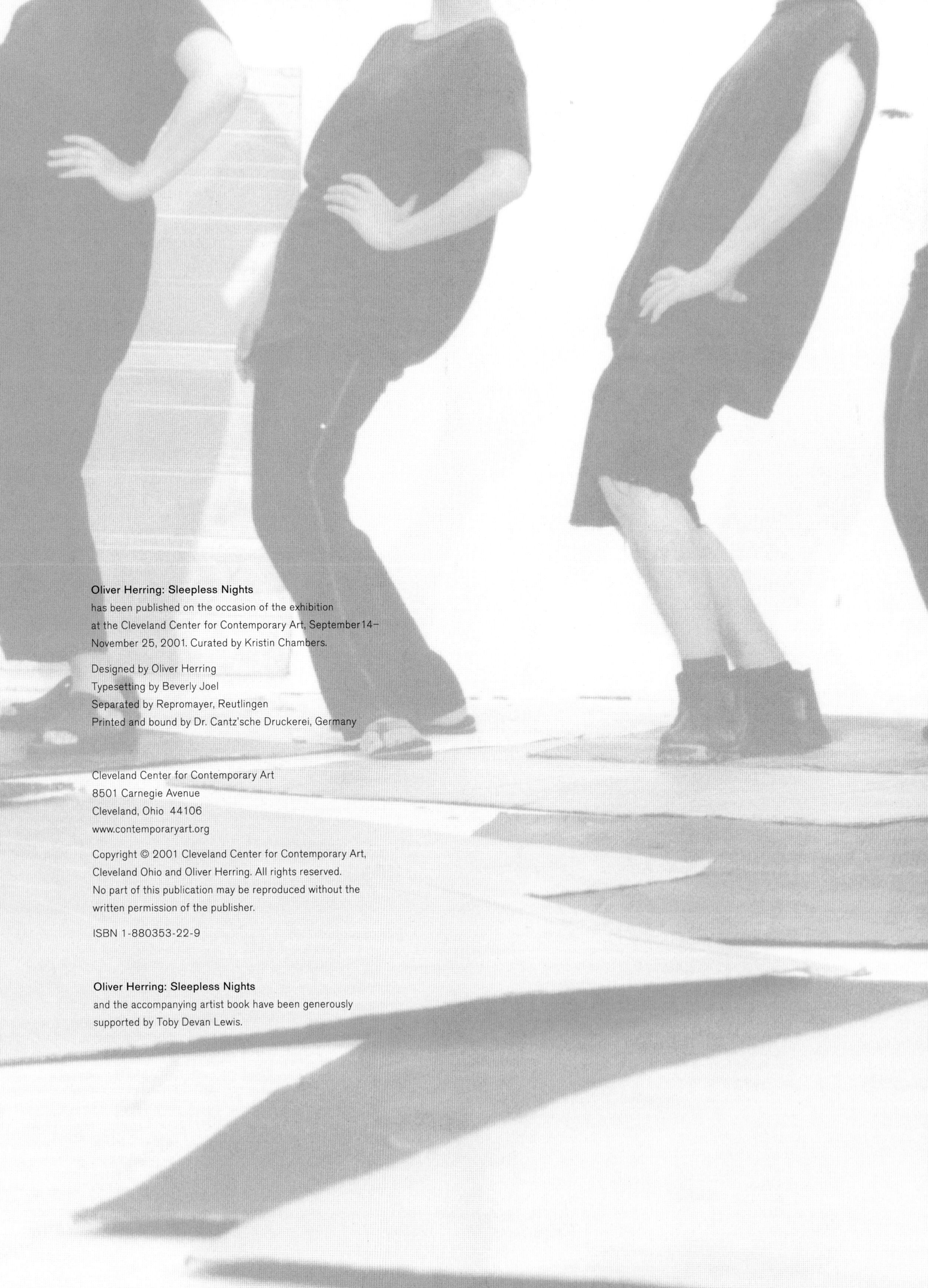

Oliver Herring: Sleepless Nights
has been published on the occasion of the exhibition
at the Cleveland Center for Contemporary Art, September 14–
November 25, 2001. Curated by Kristin Chambers.

Designed by Oliver Herring
Typesetting by Beverly Joel
Separated by Repromayer, Reutlingen
Printed and bound by Dr. Cantz'sche Druckerei, Germany

Cleveland Center for Contemporary Art
8501 Carnegie Avenue
Cleveland, Ohio 44106
www.contemporaryart.org

ISBN 1-880353-22-9

Oliver Herring: Sleepless Nights
and the accompanying artist book have been generously
supported by Toby Devan Lewis.

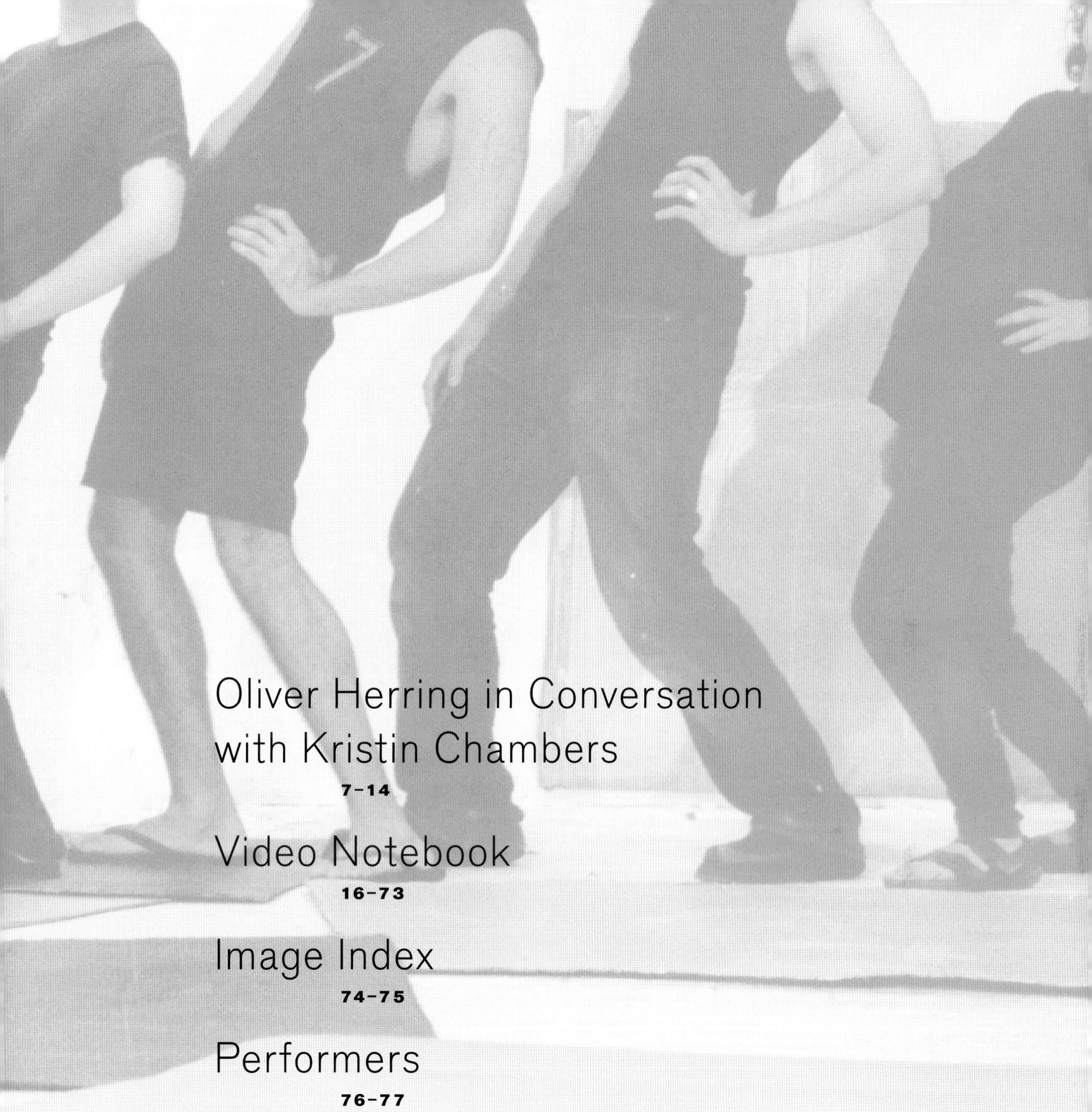

Oliver Herring in Conversation
with Kristin Chambers
7–14

Video Notebook
16–73

Image Index
74–75

Performers
76–77

Videography
78

Acknowledgements
79

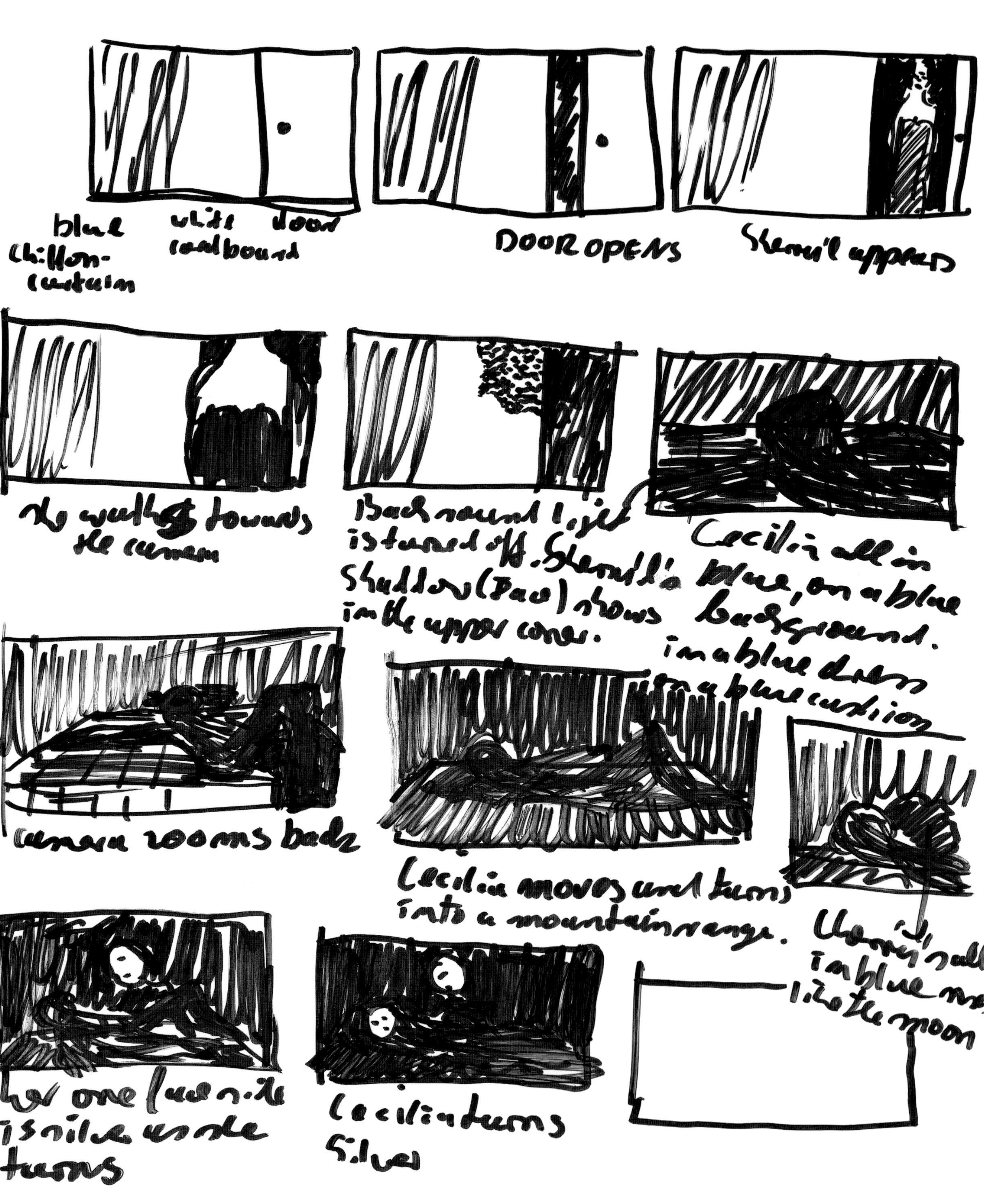

blue chiffon-curtain
white cardboard
door
DOOR OPENS
Stencil appears
she walks towards the camera
Background light is turned off. Sheroll's Shadow (Paul) shows in the upper corner.
Cecilia all in blue, on a blue background. in a blue dream on a blue cushion
camera zooms back
Cecilia moves and turns into a mountain range.
Cecilia, all in blue, like the moon
her one hand inside is smiling inside turns
Cecilia turns Silver

Oliver Herring in Conversation

WITH

Kristin Chambers

AUGUST 2001

KRISTIN CHAMBERS: Reading back through articles about your work there seems to have been a lot of discussion about how your sculptures are sad and elegiac, dealing with mortality. I know that with the work inspired by Ethyl Eichelberger there was that tone, but I have never really considered your work in that way.

OLIVER HERRING: The events of Ethyl Eichelberger's suicide helped to transpire what I did sculpturally. It was the event that made me knit. However, the knitting was really a response to his death as a life-affirming activity. It was never an act that was supposed to be morbid. I wanted to reaffirm life and knitting allowed me to do that because it is extremely time-consuming and monotonous. You mark your way from row to row, from stitch to stitch, but you have a lot of time to think about life.

KC: Was it really that conscious of a decision? Did you sit and think specifically about the medium you would use? Where you thought 'OK I need an activity that will make me slow down and think'?

OH: That really had something to do with it. I had just come to New York and I was terrified of AIDS. And here was one of my idols who died because of AIDS. In fact, he had AIDS and committed suicide. That frightened me. On the other hand, I didn't want these pieces to express sorrow or morbidity. I wanted to express my incredible appreciation of Ethyl Eichelberger as an artist, so I actually made a piece in his memory; the flower, which is not a sad piece. It seemed quite monumental. It was supposed to reflect his approach to life, which was actually quite grandiose. At the same time, it was also delicate. It sort of stemmed from there. I did think about time, and lack of time, and my own time and decided that I wanted to embark on a journey that would give me time to think. I had already played around with transparent tape, which by the way was what that flower was made from, but I had never knit before. So, I really went out to learn how to knit and thought that might be a process that could reflect the passage of time.

> **KC:** That's really interesting because you don't always find an artist who so consciously looks for the medium that would really physically, viscerally reflect the thoughts he/she is having.

OH: Well I took this very personally. I took it really hard and I felt it impacted me personally.

> **KC:** Did you know him personally?

OH: No, I never met him. That's usually the way it works with me. I just appreciate things that affect me in some way or another positively and his life did that. So when he died, I felt I wanted to give something back. At the same time this sounds more selfless than it was. I also felt I needed to move my work forward and this was an opportunity to indulge those feelings, but they were definitely feelings that I needed to explore. Up to that point my work

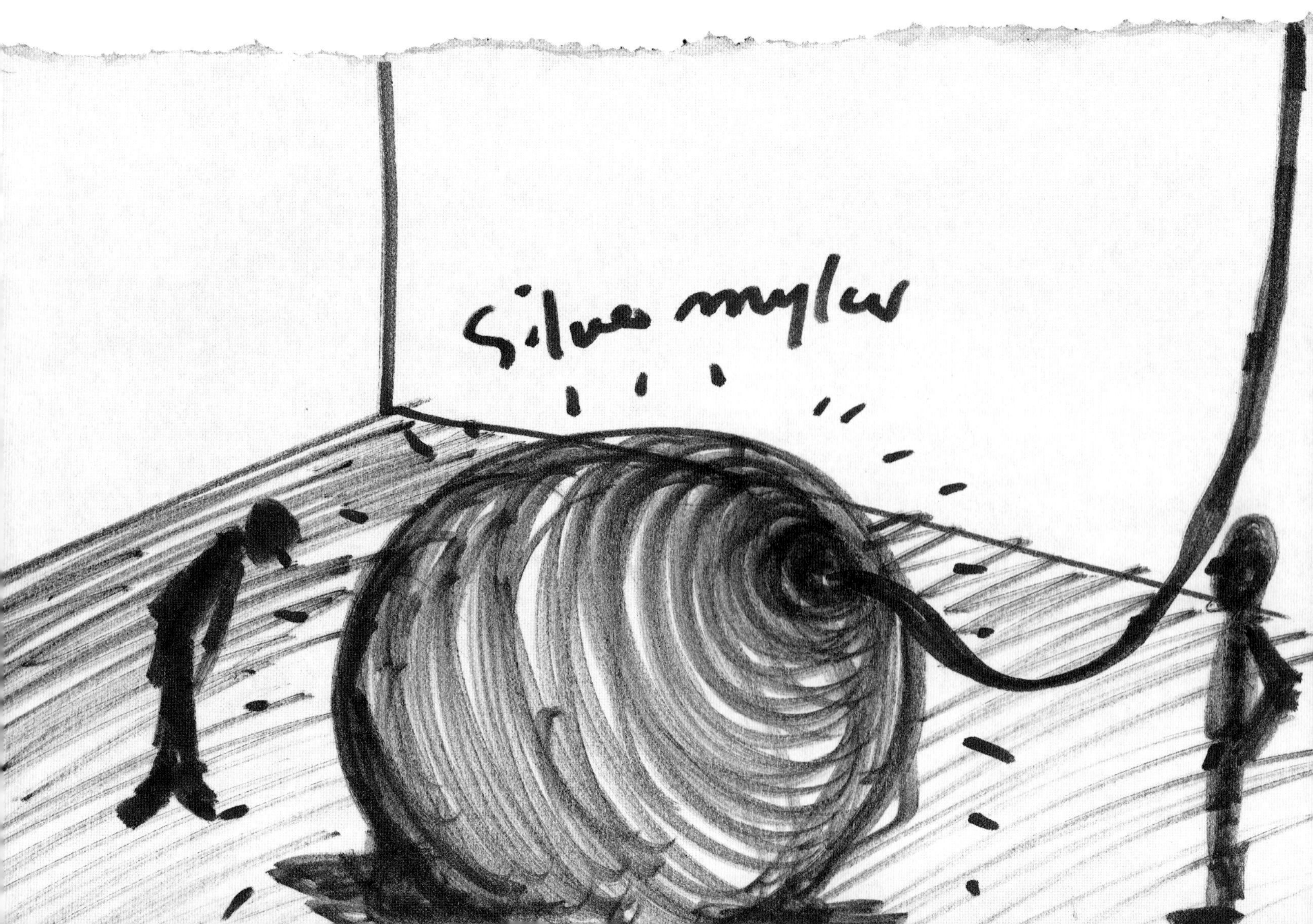

was extremely colorful. I was painting. I was making these little wild abstractions. And all of that, really from one moment to the next, just disappeared.

KC: It was really that dramatic of a shift?

OH: Yes. Not anticipated, but it was. All the color went out of my work. I couldn't look at color at all. I couldn't look at black and white. I just simply wanted transparency; something that I could project onto. Tape allowed me to do that. In fact, it was tape in combination with light that would enhance the transparency. For example, I would make a big curtain that would hang in front of a window. It was less a curtain as much as a sheet and what I wanted was to have the daylight make an imprint and leave a trace of a place and of a time. Over time that outline would disappear again, but for a while it was definitely there. I tried to be really ephemeral and abstract. Non-committal.

KC: Where is that flower?

OH: The flower is in my possession. One of the few pieces that I never gave away.

KC: In talking about knitting, how do you feel about all the implications of craft and women's work and sentimentality?

OH: Well, I embarked on this whole thing very innocently not being too burdened by any of the implications. However, after a few months went by and I was still knitting (which I hadn't planned on), I started to get worried. I thought 'boy I have been to school and here I sit knitting, is this really necessary?' And I also felt it was really very emasculating.

I consider it performance art above all. When all of this happened, activism-especially AIDS activism-was really pronounced in New York. When I went to undergraduate school, which was where I started to knit my sculpture, ACT UP was really active and I was aware of and moved by that. But to go out on the street and demonstrate or to join a group has never really been my style. So, I considered this sort of a private form of activism. To do something intense and learn from it in order to change something in me and then use that sort of energy, from whatever I learned, and apply it to something productive. I started in the studio by transforming this mundane, accessible material and turned it into something that was meaningful to me. Which really went to the heart of what Ethyl Eichelberger had done. Not just him, his whole circle-Charles Ludlum, The Ridiculous Theatrical Company… Their performances would consist of making meaningful situations happen through very, very mundane means.

KC: So, that is the part of it that you've carried with you?

OH: Yes, and I think it had a major impact on the way I make my videos, too. Not so much the videos themselves, but the way I make my sets and costumes. As you know, there is nothing very high-tech about them. They are very handcrafted and made mostly with recy-

9

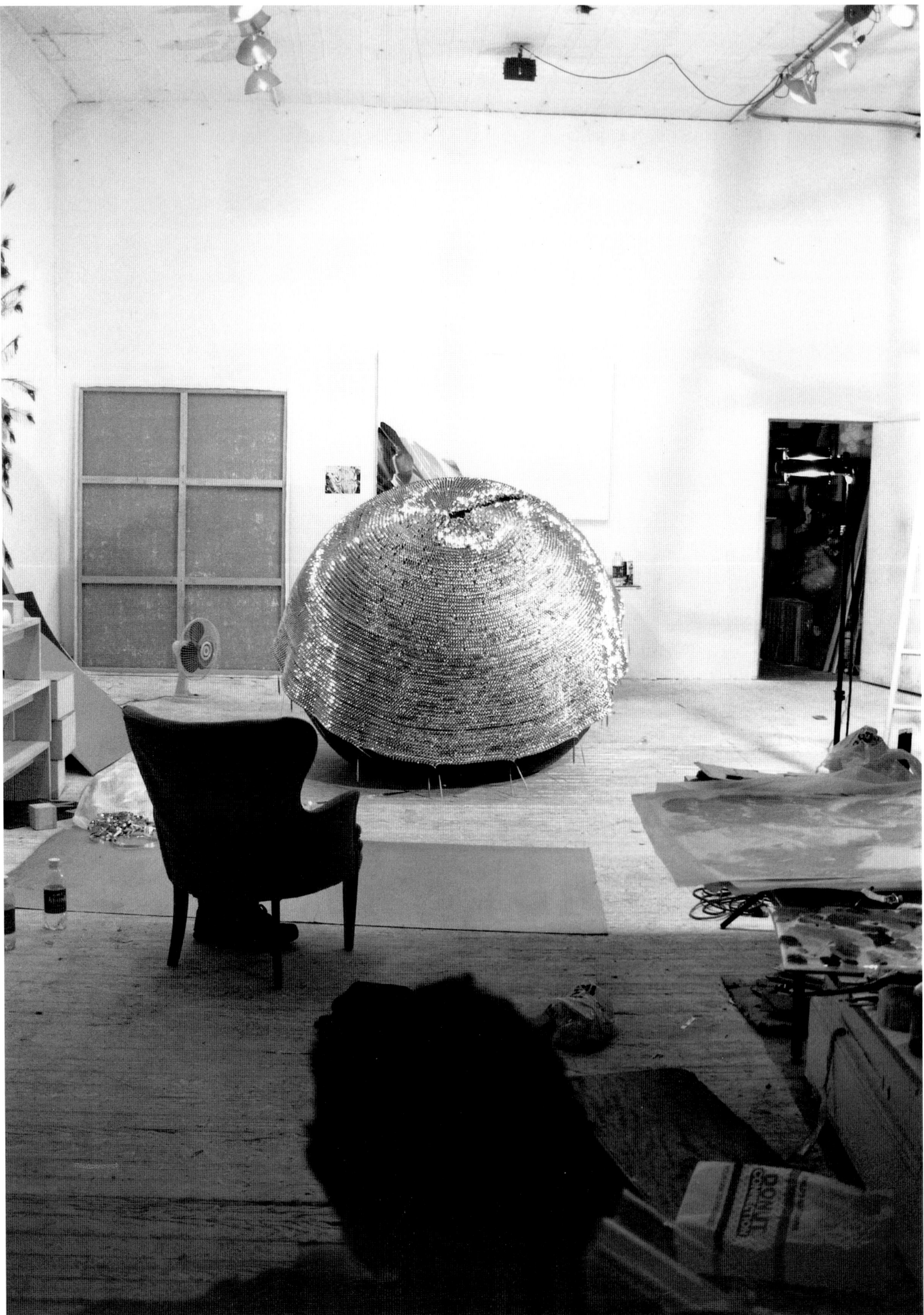

cled cardboard. I have used those same 15, 20 sheets for just about every single one of my videos. So that sense of being extremely economical and resourceful is something I found really inspiring about those guys.

KC: That's really interesting to me-knitting is such an exacting, like you said, very mundane, very repetitive, very solitary activity. And then the way you make your videos is collaborative, and loose, and whatever happens happens. Really so opposite of the process of knitting.

OH: The video came at a point where I really needed something to contrast my sculpture and process with. As you said, knitting can be extremely repetitive and sometimes truly boring. I also felt it only expressed a part of my personality and I was looking for another medium through which I could express maybe another side of my personality. Film, or video, seemed appropriate because, for one thing, formally it is really close to knitting.

KC: How so?

OH: It is extremely incremental and made up of little moments.

KC: And you do stop motion.

OH: And I do stop motion, which...

KC: ...makes it even more incremental.

OH: Makes it even more incremental...exactly. So, formally, it was close to what I was doing anyway. On the other hand, when I make a sculpture...once it's conceived then the rest of the process is more or less just hacking my way through it, executing it. Actually this is not always the case. There are some pieces where I challenge myself throughout the process. Where I lay these booby traps along the way and I have to be on my toes all the time.

KC: It's funny to hear you talk about the video expressing another side of your personality because when I came to your work it was really through an early video (not the sculptures). It was so whimsical, and funny, and charming, and quirky, and strange. When I realized — I couldn't believe it was the same person. It has since come to make perfect sense, but at first the sculptures seemed to me so formal and meticulous.

OH: They were always deliberately motionless. They were about passivity some were supposed to be really gravity-bound, others in a state of being in between something, instead of being concrete. They felt so minimal and they gave me a lot of space to project onto. Most of the motion or activity that happened with these sculptures was up to the viewer.

The videos started out as flights of fancy. I wanted to express a lot of things that I had not intentionally suppressed but that were suppressed through the discipline that was self-imposed in these sculptures. In the last few years these things started to break through and spill over onto the sculpture. Restlessness — the figures started to turn colorful and I started to express motion. Some of these are my favorite pieces.

KC: Mine too — I love that red crouching figure.

OH: Me too. But you know I just came to a point where I felt like there was a lot that needed to pop out and it would take me years just to finish a sculpture that would express what I wanted to express. So I felt like I needed to add a more immediate medium. Little did I know that stop-motion video is just as excruciating as knitting, but as I said, I leave it open so that I still don't know what I am going to embark on the morning when I start. And you can testify to that-I gave you some sense of what I wanted to do for this video in Cleveland and I maybe started out that way-the first shots might resemble that to some degree-but as soon as I saw these people (the actors) and the blue, the materials, the props in front of me it just went off in a totally different direction and I just responded to the moment.

KC: That's what's great about video. You have talked about the sculptures as sort of marking time-you are knitting into a work the events and thoughts that are happening as you make a piece. A video also marks time, but it marks what happens in the studio with other people around you and that is what is woven into the video.

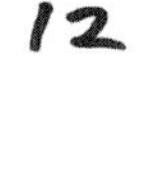

OH: You're right. It's very communal. If I can't go out into the world, I have to bring the world into my studio, which is basically the way I sometimes have to conduct a good part of my social life since my work is so time consuming. I have to bring my friends over, or sometimes people that interest me who I actually don't know that well. And that is how I get to know them. The videos are time-consuming. One session can easily take from morning to very late at night and the unusual circumstances tend to make these situations very intimate and really fun to share with others.

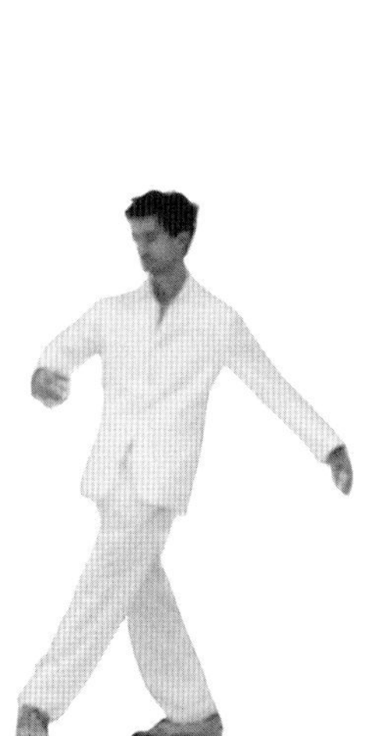
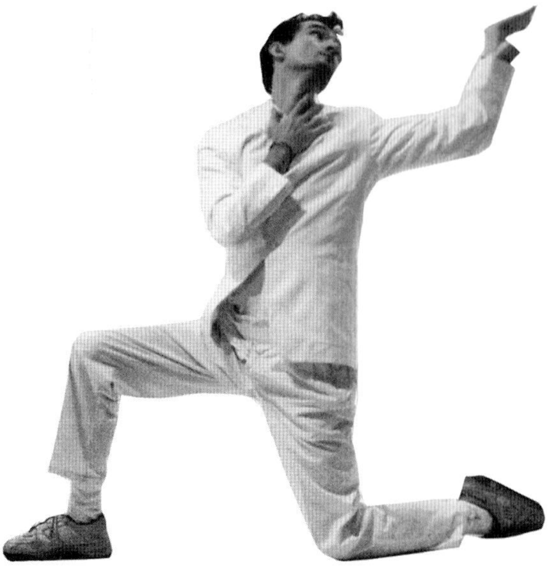
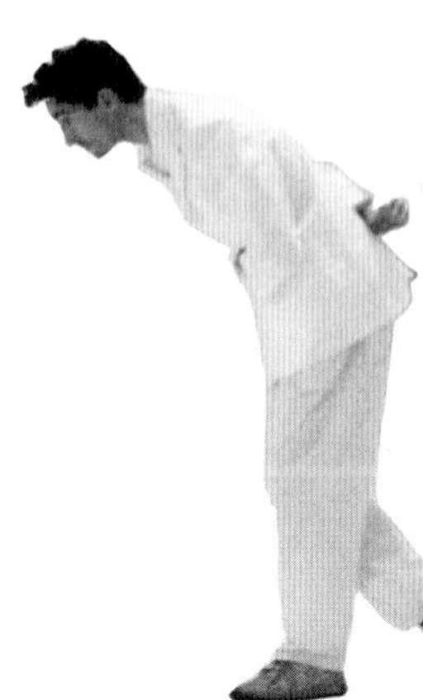

 Why have you stuck with stop-motion?

OH: Well, it helps me to manipulate the action from one moment to the next. Since stop-motion is made one image at a time, I can change things in-between shots. Some of the people that really interest me in terms of what I am doing filmically are Buster Keaton, Laurel and Hardy, and Charlie Chaplin; people right at the beginning of filmmaking. I am fascinated by the performance quality of what these guys did. Their imagination was not limited by what was feasible at all. Quite the opposite and they found ways to make things happen. Any situation. If one of these guys wanted to fly or if Stan Laurel lost a hat and he wanted it to land exactly next to Oliver Hardy, they had to find a way to make this happen and they found ways. Very often you'll see the string that is tied to the hat. I find that very charming and it relates directly to what I am doing. I am very interested in finding hands-on, immediate, and creative solutions to express whatever I want to express and I try not to limit myself to anything. If I want to fly in a video, I find ways to do that. It is often very labor intensive, but I am not interested in relying on computer technology or the latest software.

KC: What about the role of narrative in your videos? I have heard you talk about starting with a script, but I don't imagine that it is a script in the traditional sense of the word. Do you start with some kind of narrative and then let it fall apart?

OH: It depends on the video really. I have started with scripts in the past, but I have always abandoned them. And I have started with scripts in a very sincere way before I realized that I would have to abandon them.

KC: Did they have actual stories?

OH: They would be very stream-of-consciousness. For example, Exit–where I am flying through the air… I had sort-of scripted that. On the other hand, that was the one video that was in direct response to what I daydream about when I sit in my yellow armchair in the studio knitting.

KC: You dream about flying?

13

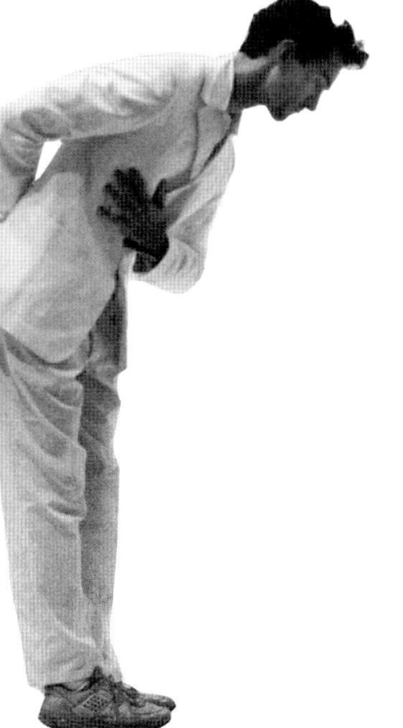

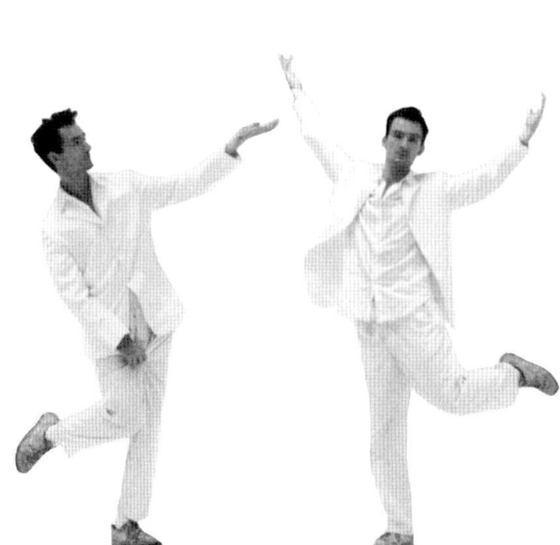

OH: I guess. Flying to Mozart's Queen of the Night or whatever. The video is slightly erotically charged. There is a wet, red looking jungle that is vaguely based on a Rousseau painting and you have my sort-of megalomaniacal scene of 20 Olivers dancing with each other and me sitting in the chair flying, turning somersaults out of restlessness or whatever. I don't want to read too much into the video, but it was all very pent up and needed to pop out.

I usually have a look or a mood I want to express or certain formal features that I want to explore further. For example, I have been playing around with phosphorescence. I have also been trying to make some of my videos extremely painterly. I try to exploit the stop-motion vehicle to basically paint one still life at a time or construct one sculpture at a time.

> **KC:** I find that the best way to describe many of the videos is to call them "moving paintings."

OH: Yes. That and/or changing sculptures. It sort of depends on where my head is. In some I am painting away and in others sculpture is really at the forefront. In others yet, it's really performance art or body art or vaudeville or dance. It depends on my mood, the overall atmosphere, and what goes through my head.

> **KC:** When we first started talking about doing the project at the Center and you were thinking about a new video, you were describing to me a solitary scene where a woman on a bed in a dark room would slowly awake and rise as the room changed from dark to light colors and then would slowly descend back to sleep as dark fell again. It would be a very short, simple piece. And now...?

OH: (laughs) Well, now it is a grand production number, something out of an Esther Williams movie. Sometimes I start grand and I end up focusing on one person and everyone sits there terribly bored, or the opposite happens, I start with one person and 14 people end up in the film. I think at this point, some of the people in this particular video have been in a lot of my videos and I am starting to know how to work with them, which makes it really tempting to use them. Also, I think I always shy away from my original idea. Maybe because of the way I make sculpture, I don't like following through with ideas too closely. I find it very claustrophobic to just follow a concept. It becomes all about the idea without expressing anything more than the idea. I find a lot of video work restrictive and not that generous. It doesn't offer me anything that I want to know about beyond technical matters.

What I think I am interested in in my videos is to express myself through them, through all sorts of tricks and means, by using people and props and architecture and god knows what else. Basically they are slices of my mind. Not that that is more interesting than an idea, but it is more complex for me because I am trying to figure out what the hell they mean. And I also find it more entertaining because the viewer will never know what lies around the corner if I don't even know what lies around the corner. It's like a journey through the feeble mind. It's never predictable.

KC: What about the role of music in the videos?

OH: Totally integral. I usually have a piece of music in mind, not a whole piece of music, just samples that I turn into my own. You can never tell what the source is. The way I sample sound is as primitive and crude as the way I make the films. I usually sit with my camcorder in front of the stereo and map out sequences and beats I like and record.

KC: Let's go back to the sculpture for a minute. It seems that much of your previous sculptural work was fairly figurative. Then you talked about wanting to break out of the constraints of the sculpture and used video to do that. It seems that now the sculptures are becoming more minimal and abstract. Do you think that the video served as such a good outlet that you are now able to be more minimal again?

OH: I think that is partly true. About two years ago I slipped a disc in my neck and couldn't knit for a long time. So, I actually sidetracked to video and I was really happy to do that. Yes, I released a lot of things in the video that I probably would have projected onto my sculpture. But over that time I also had the chance to think about what makes my sculptures potent. I think for these pieces that I made for Cleveland, my mind is in a place where I just want to focus on the process of how these works are made. The roundness of these sculptures lends inevitability to the process, almost like these things never stop. It feels never ending. To me, the new pieces are not really abstract and my previous work was not exactly recognizable and figurative. I can't see the sculptures without seeing the process that made them.

The new works almost resemble cushions and mattresses and sheets. For various reasons, I have had a hard time sleeping this summer and it started to get to me physically. Every time I drew a sketch it started to look like a sheet or mattress or cushion, but always stressed-never relaxed. They always had a bend, a twist, a wave or a curve. The sculptures have the waves and curves knit into them. They may seem simple, but they are quite complicated. You think you get it, but when you take a second look you see all the distortions that make you question what you see in the first place. They always come back to what you want to see in them, about your own experience, which is mostly narrative and figurative.

SLEEPLES NIGHTS VIDEO NOTEBOOK

A FREE FORM FLIGHT
INTO MY VIDEOS AND MY SCULPTURE

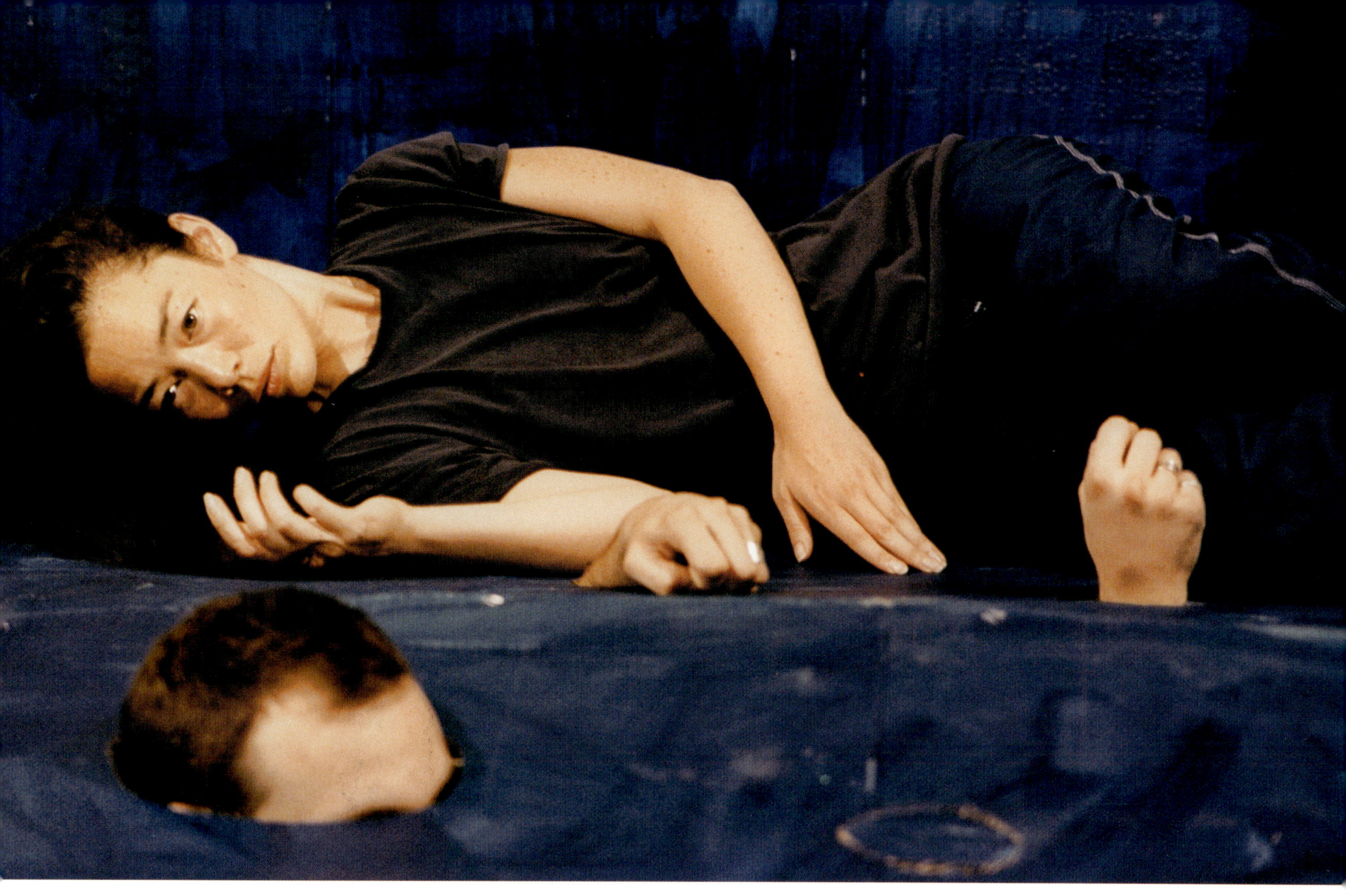

One of two opening scenes from "Sleepless Nights", a video made up of two interacting performances. Both sequences start out blue and eventually turn gold.

"Videosketch #5" was shot as an experiment when I bought my camera. It is shot like a negative, light is dark and dark is light, and it is the only video I made that is not stop-motion. In it I projected the shadow of myself crouching on a pedestal against the corner of two walls.

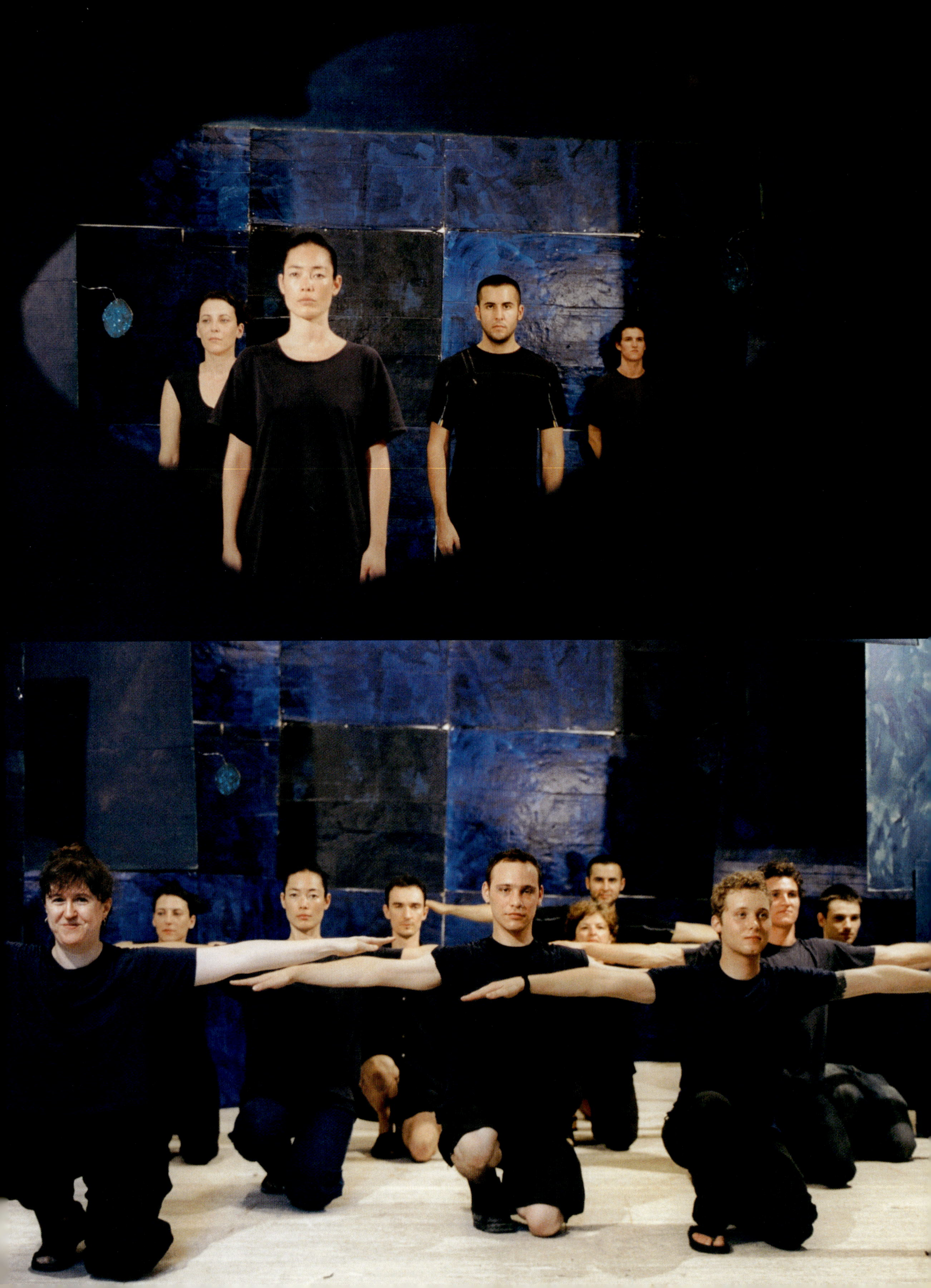

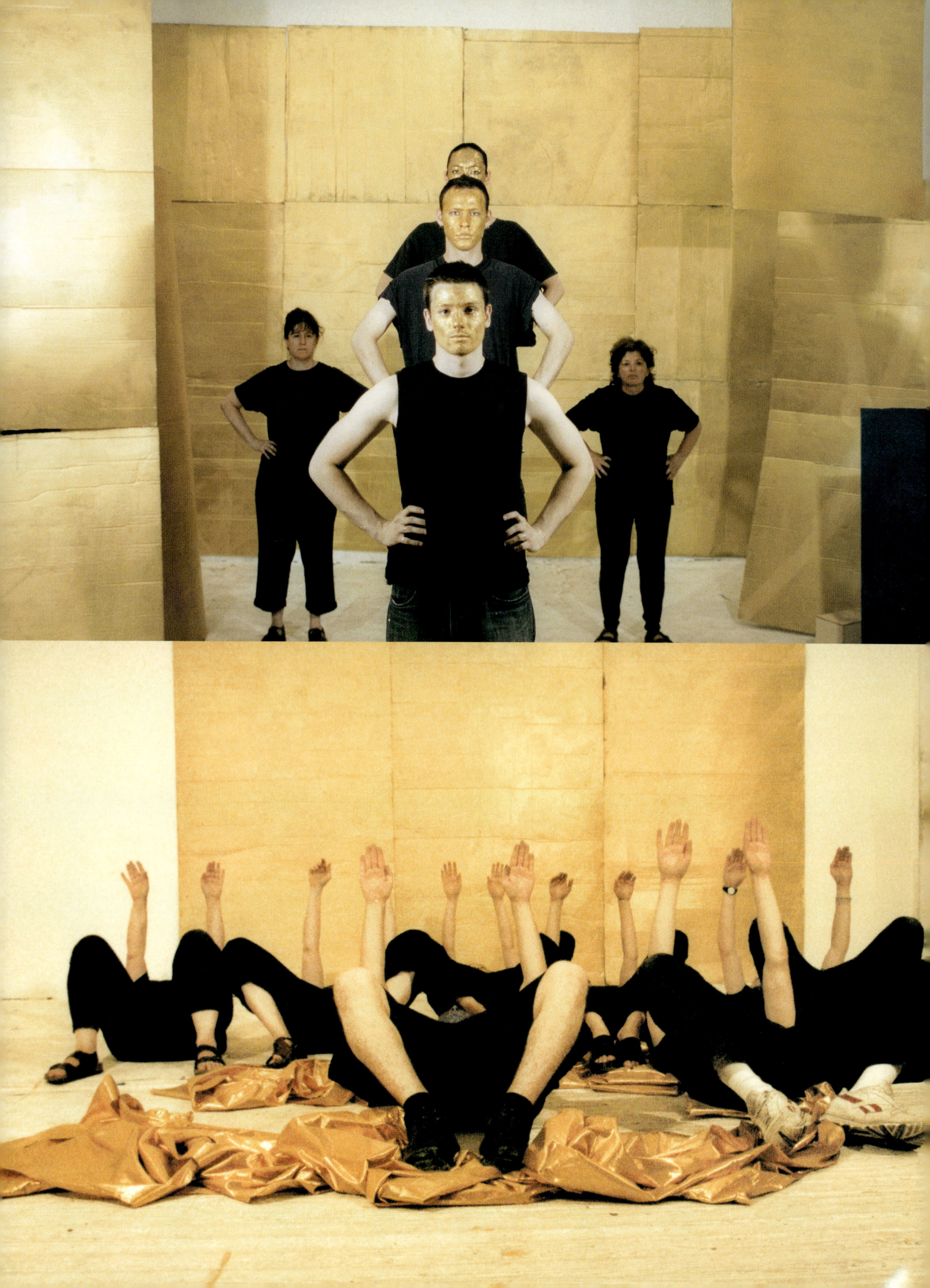

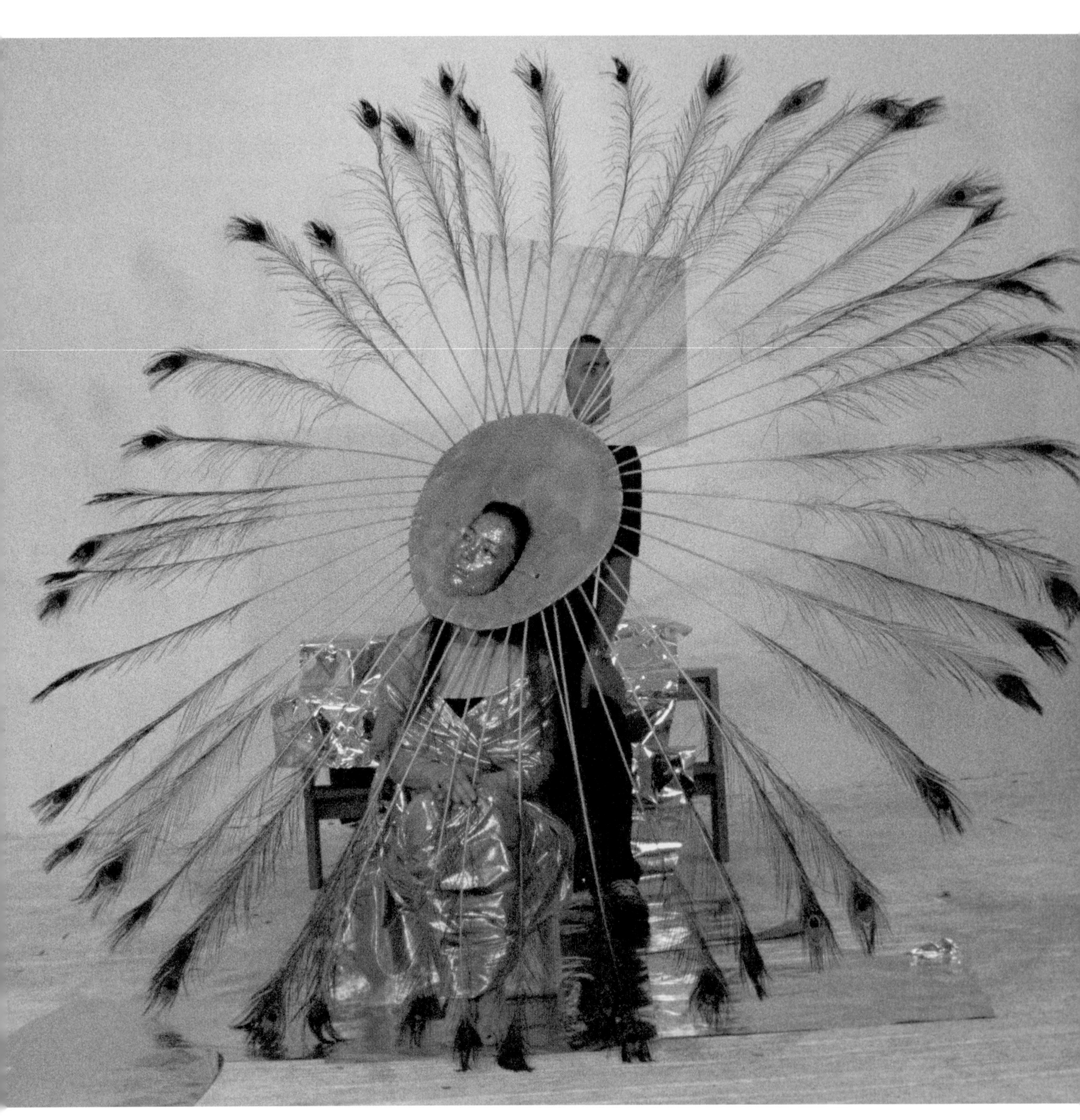

One of the closing shots of "Sleepless Nights". The round motion, a theme used in my new sculpture, was carried over into the video. The headdress is introduced two feathers at a time.

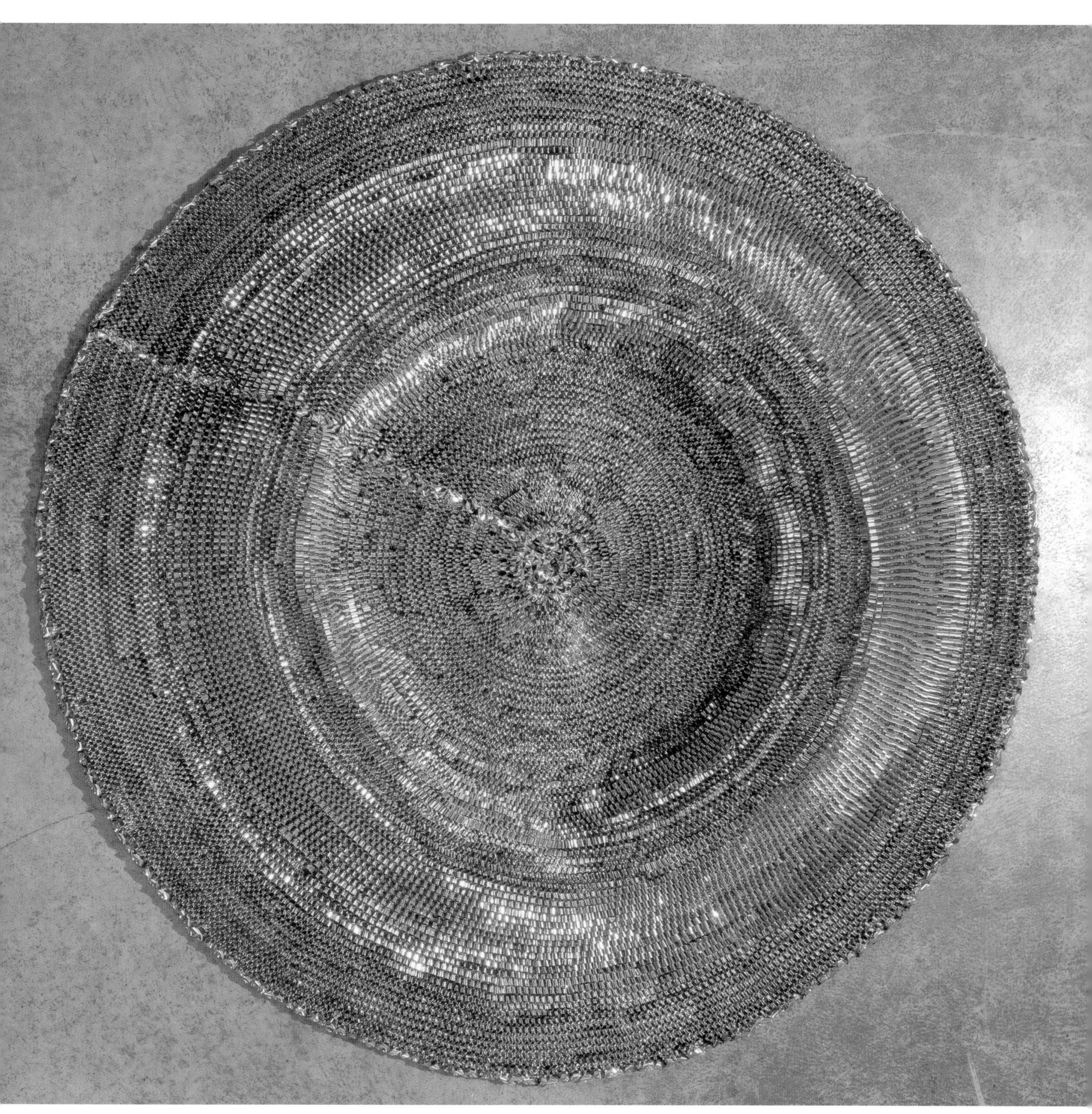

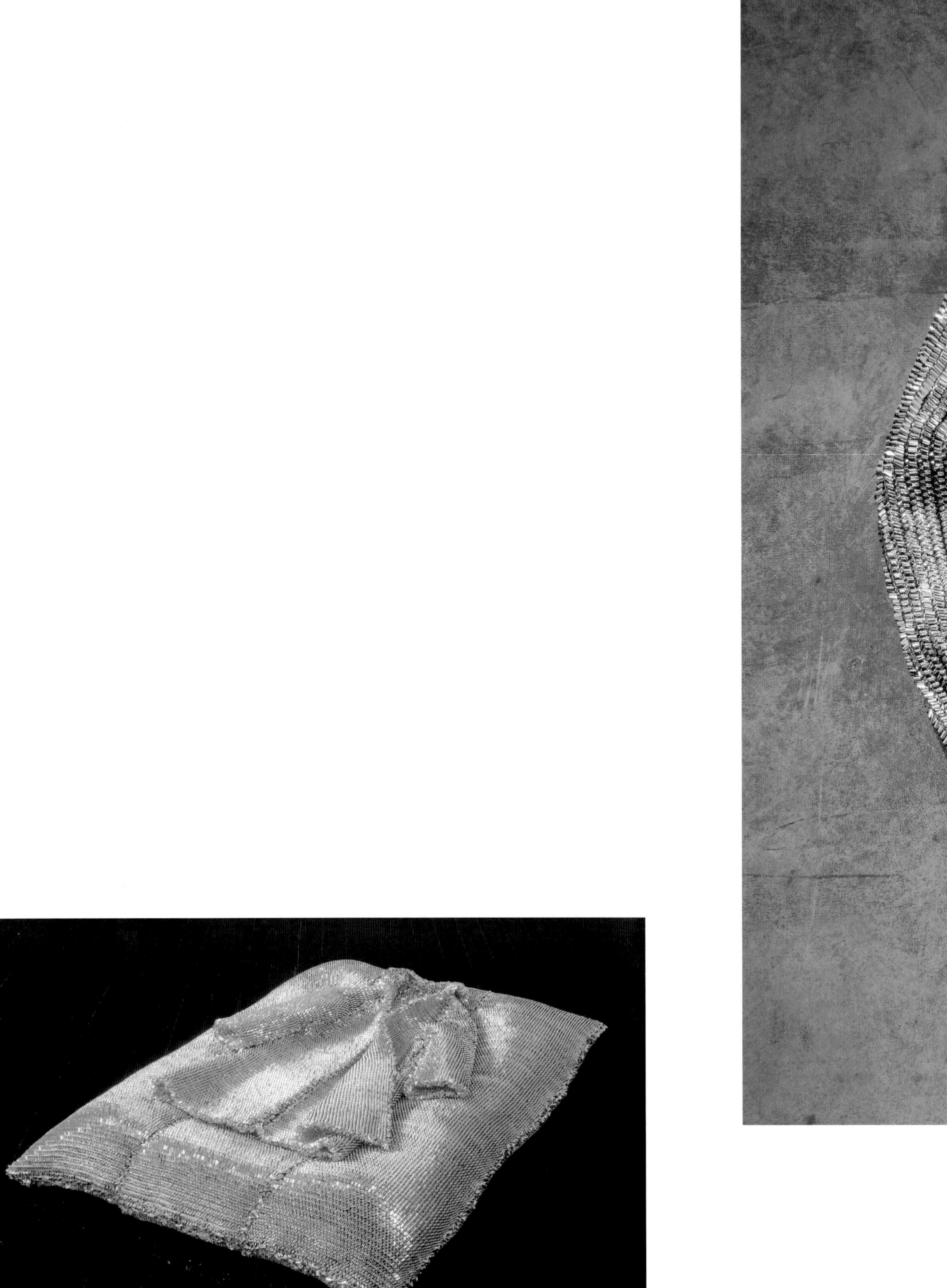

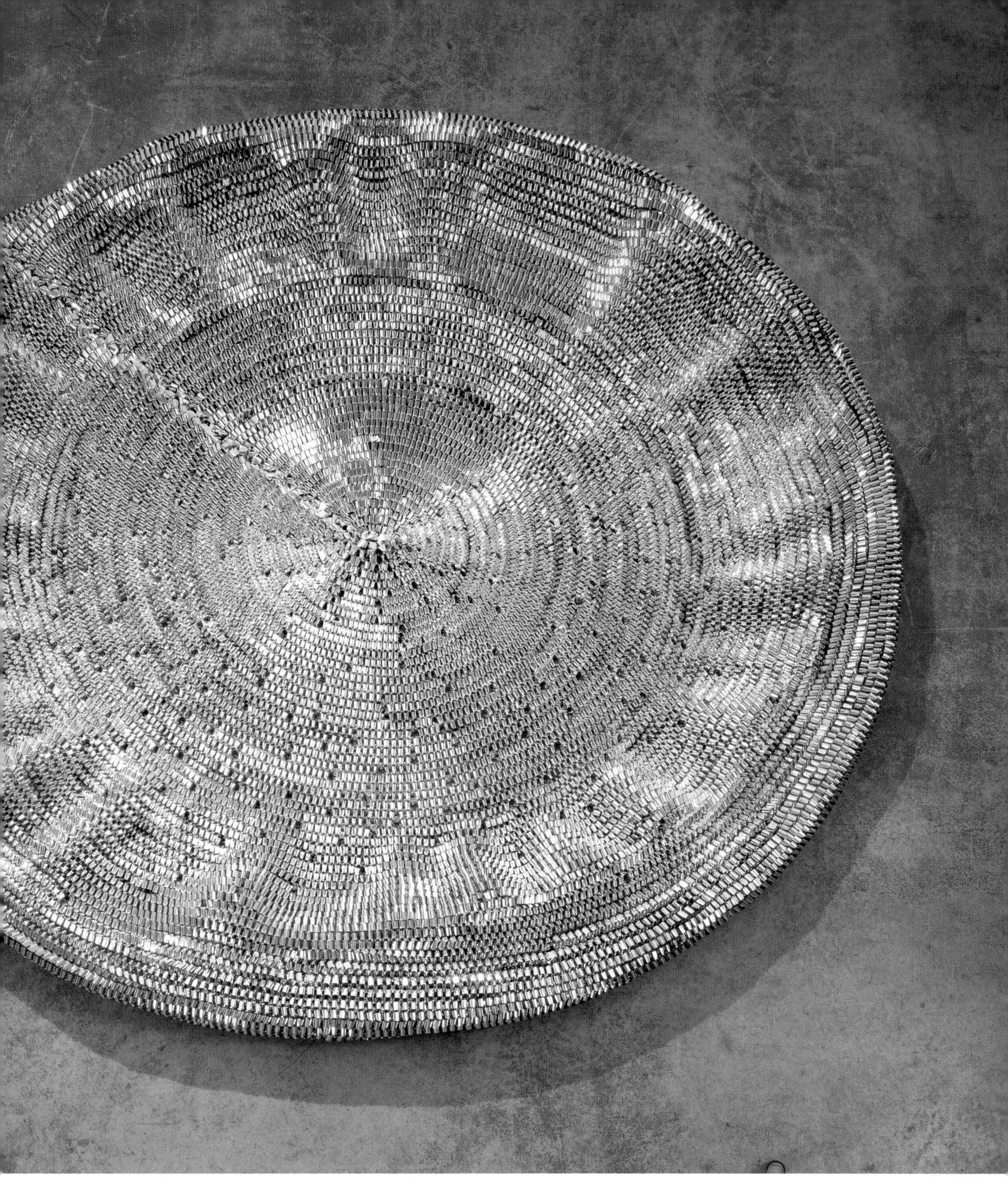

"Distorted Round #1, (2001)
and one of my earliest pieces
"Queensize bed with Coat", (1993-4)

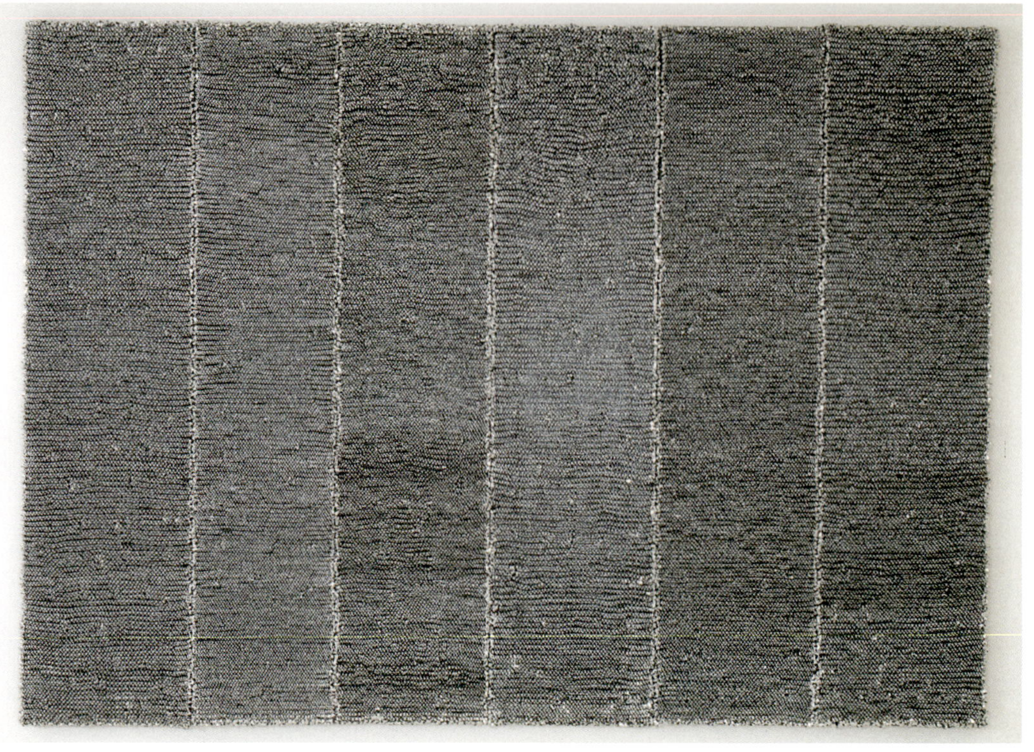

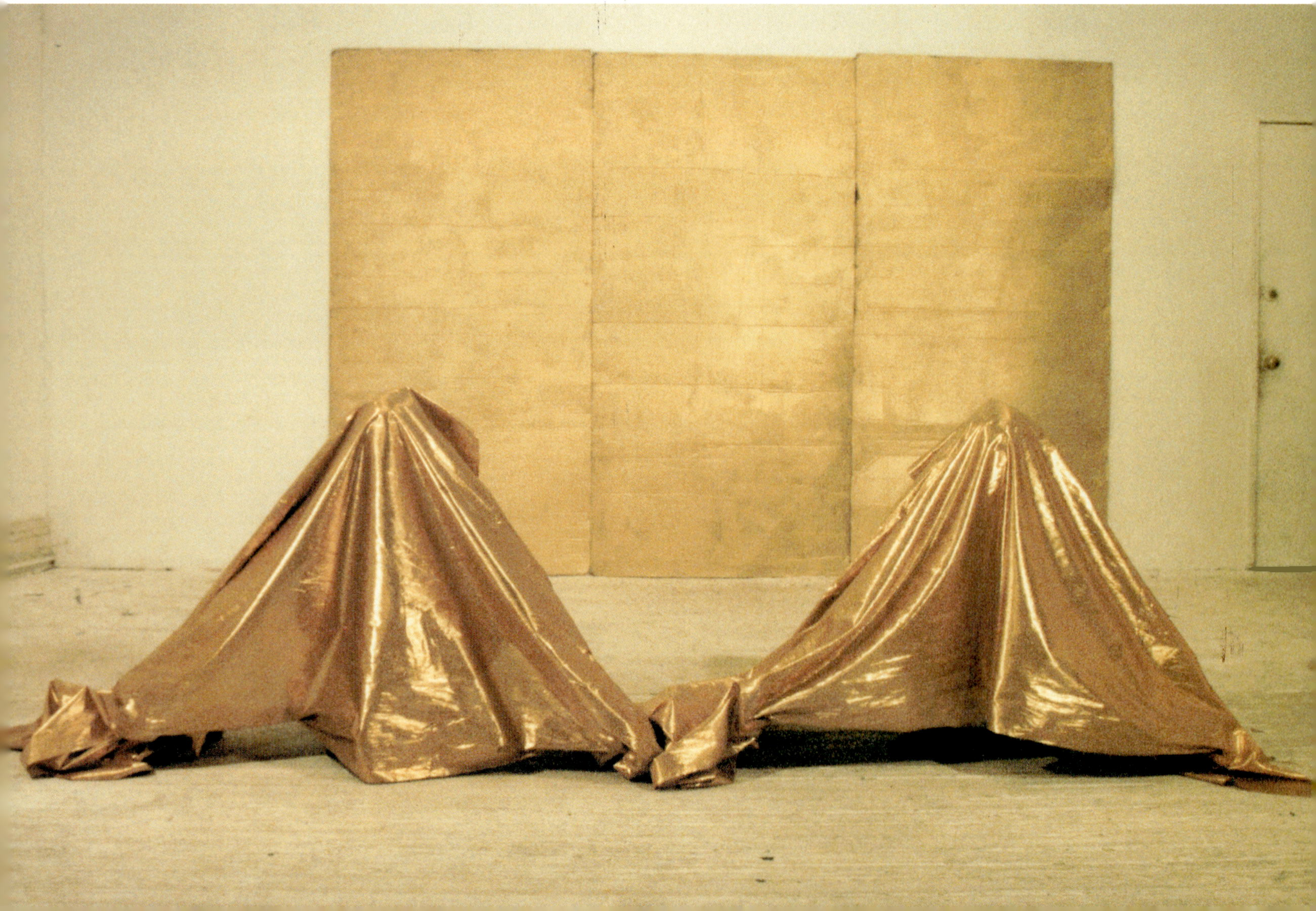

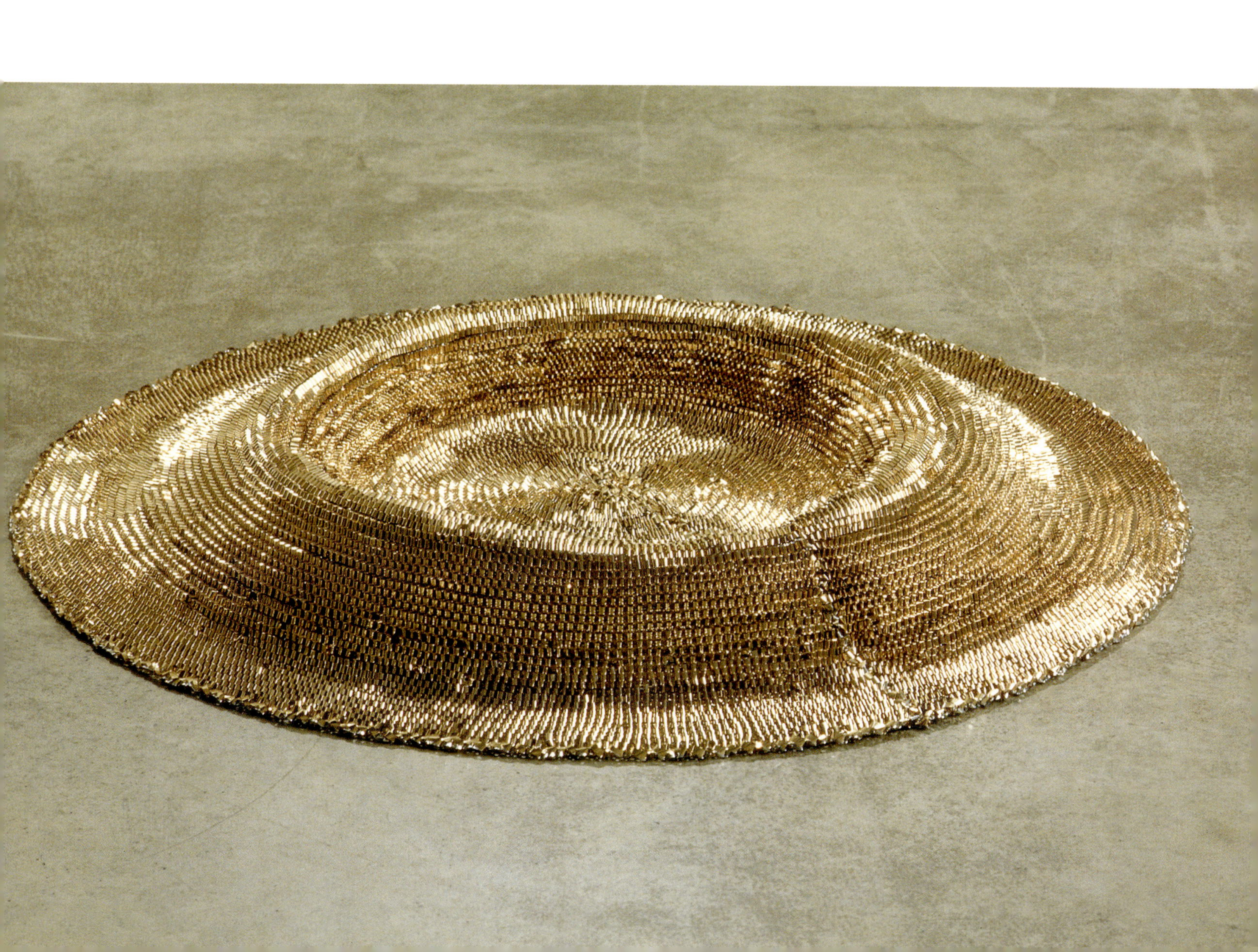

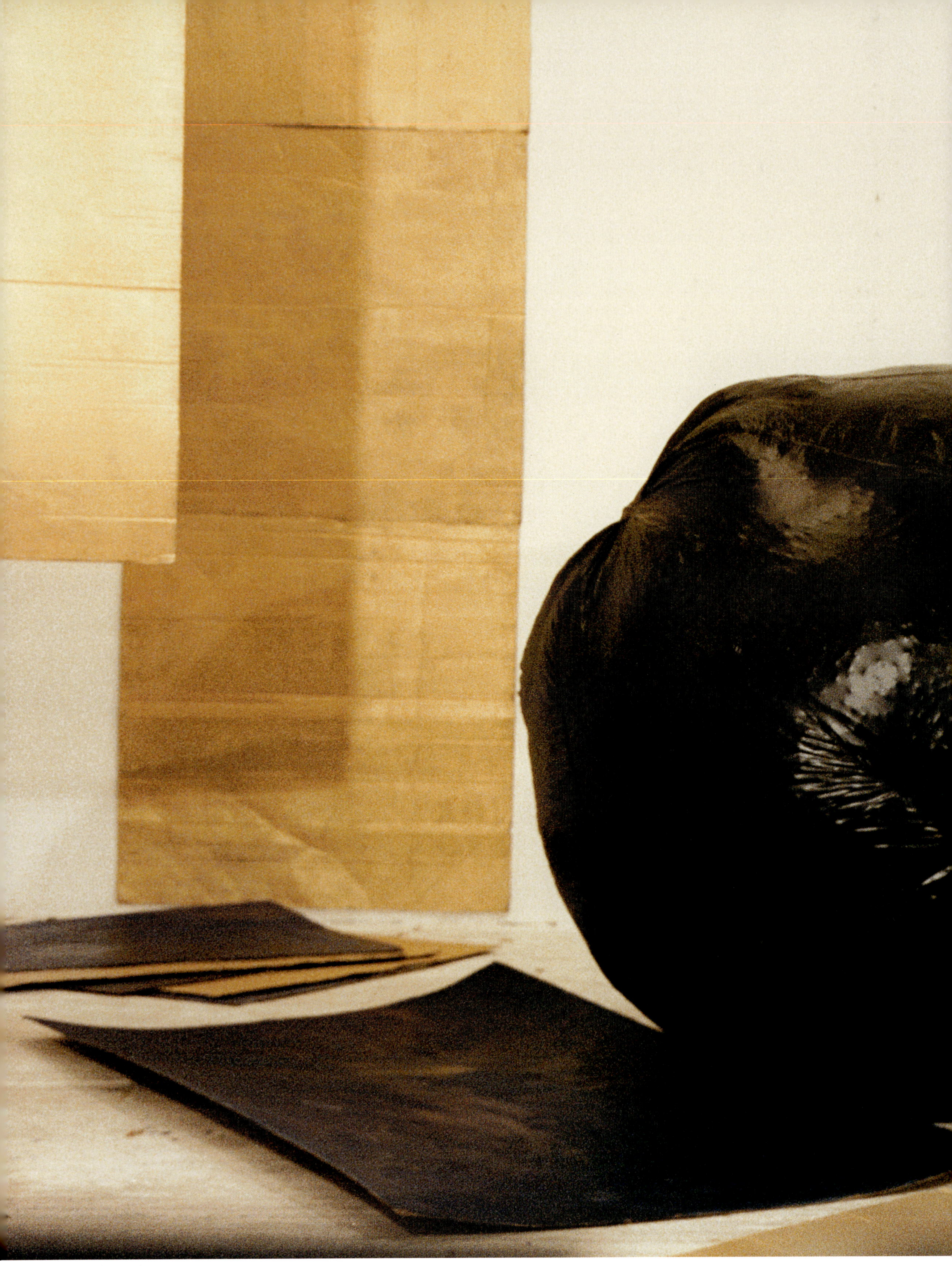

The ball-like structure is a life-size maquette for "Big Round Flat".

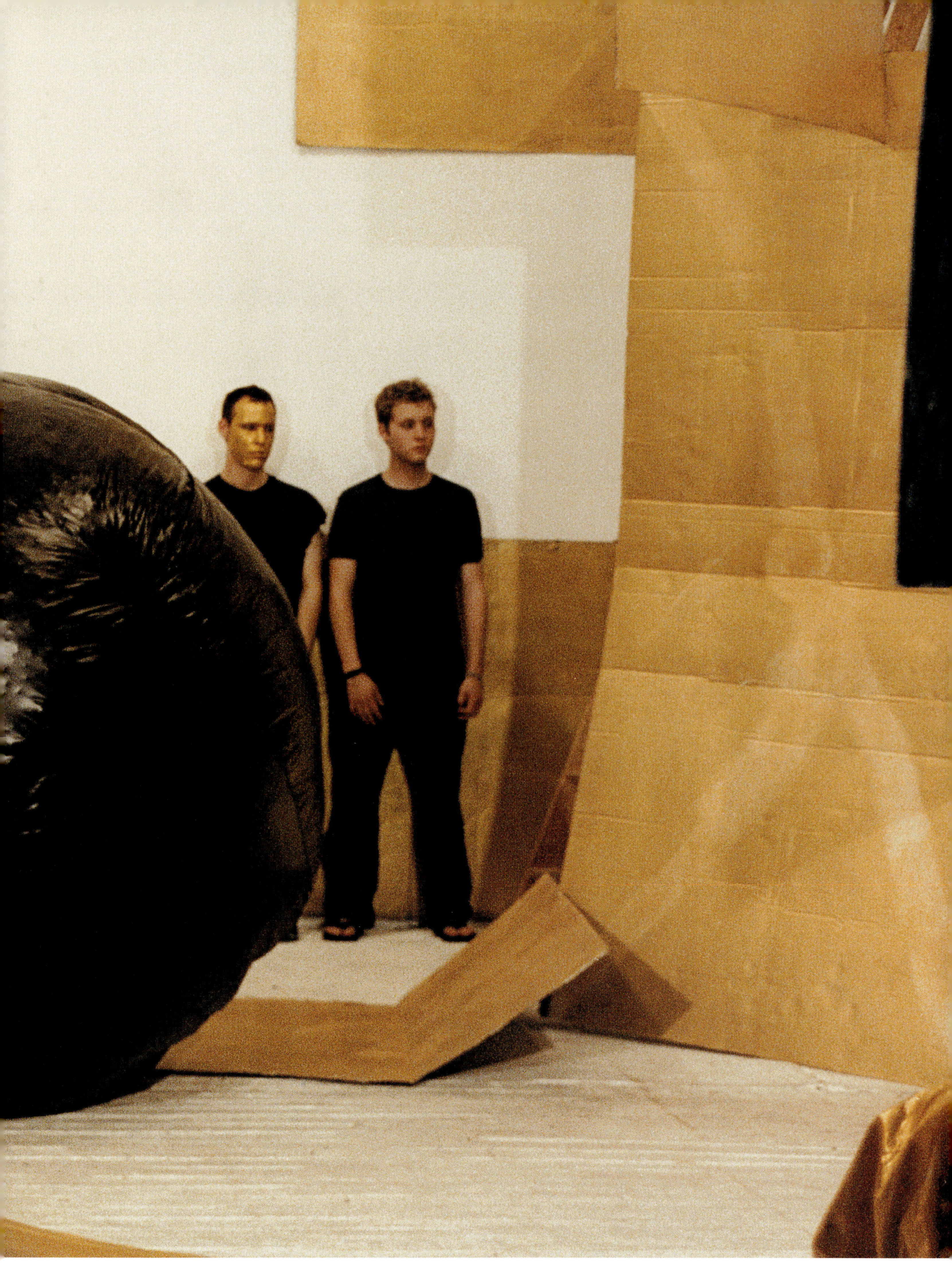

It rolled it's weight into the video.

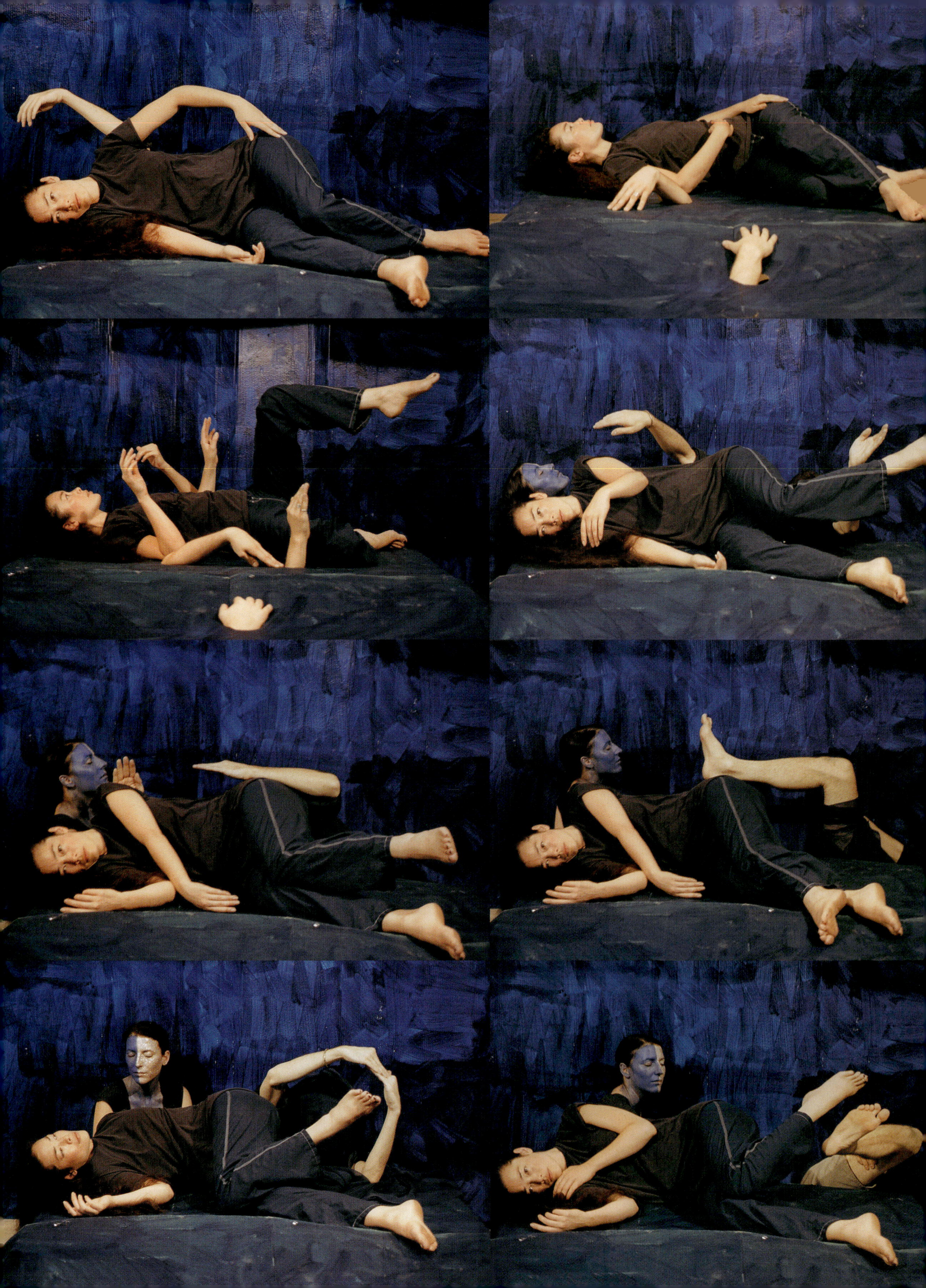

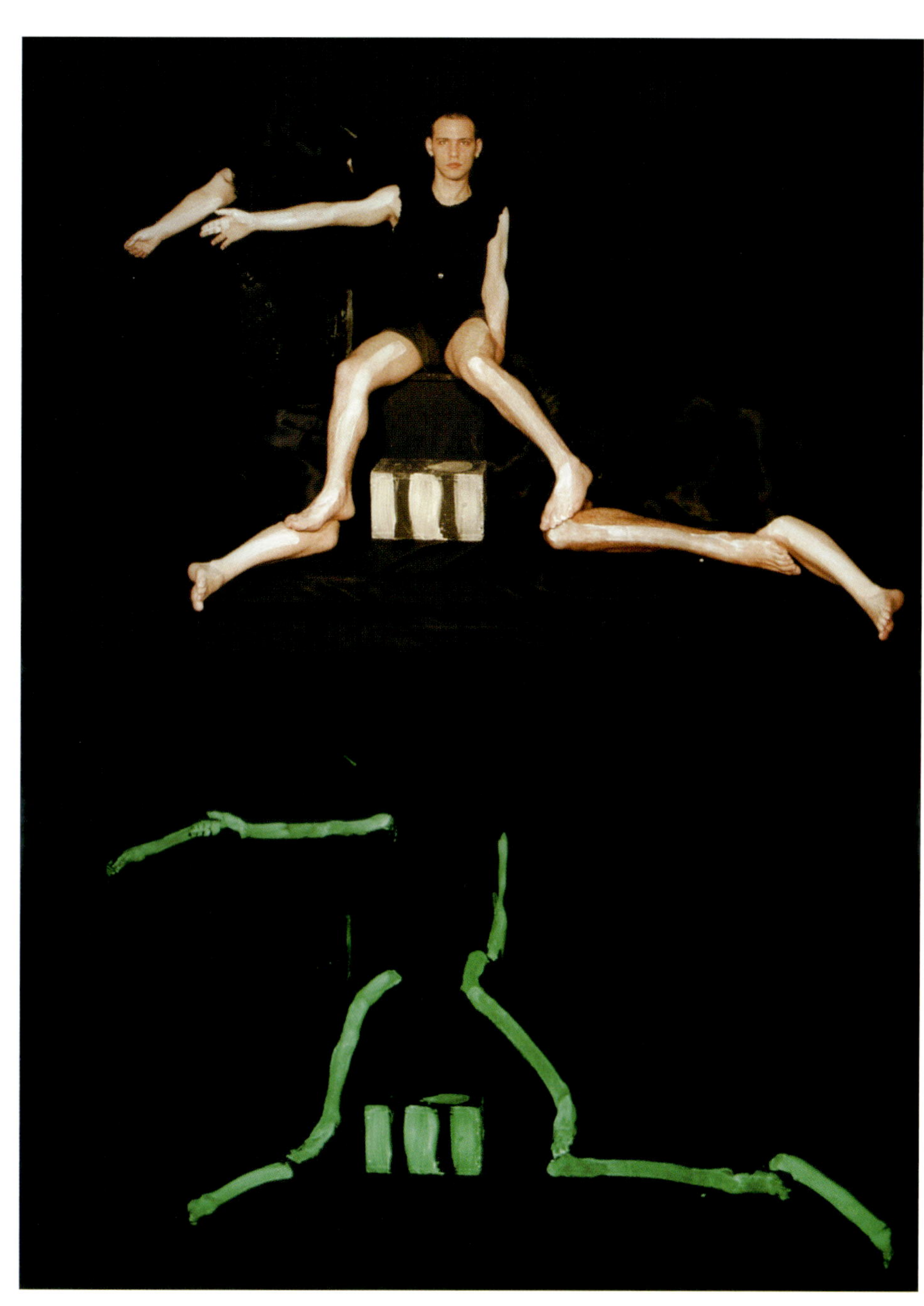

"Sleepless Nights" (left) shares its vocabulary with many of my earlier videos like this sequence from "Little Dances of Misfortunes", also 2001.

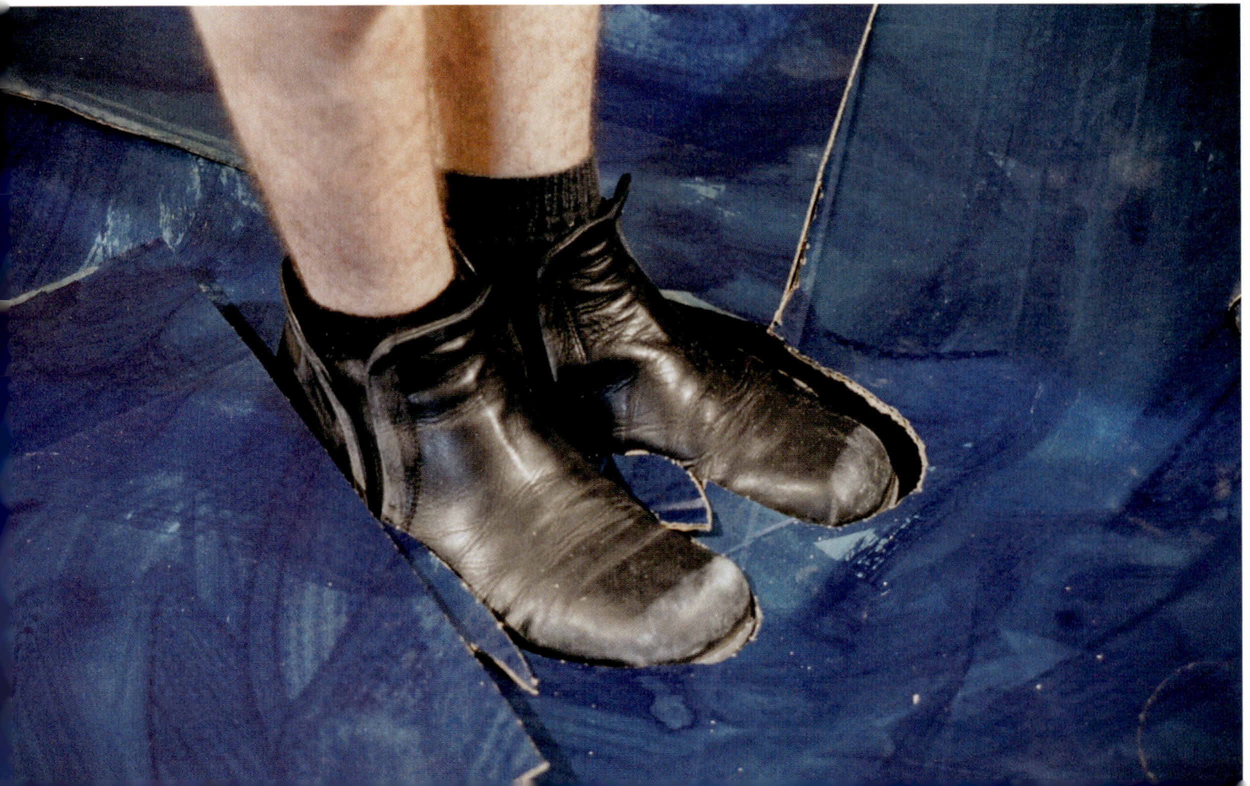

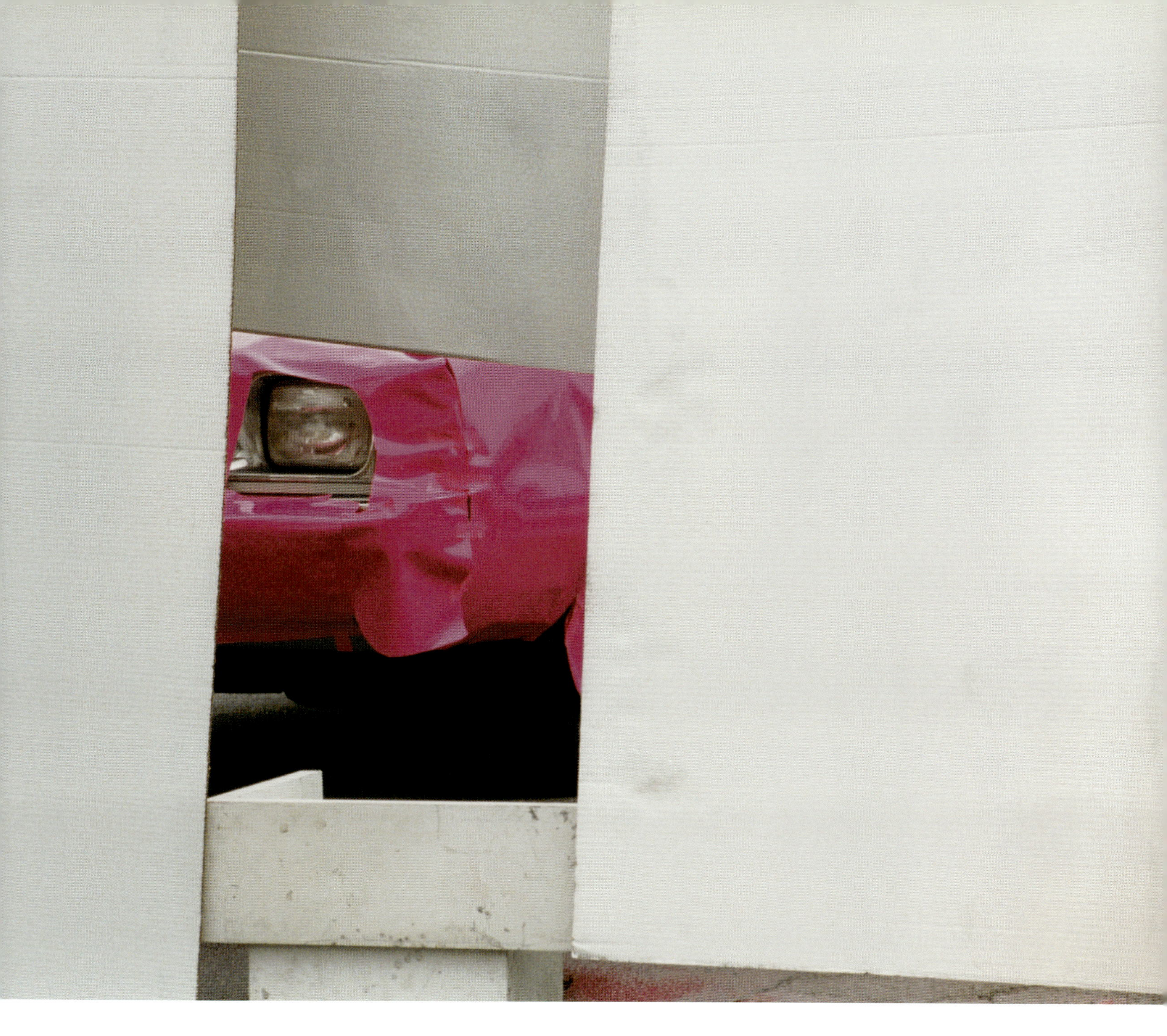

Two instances of makeshift creativity,
one from "Sleepless Nights" and one
from "Pure Sublimation", (2000).

I have recycled these same twenty
sheets of cardboard throughout almost
all of my videos.

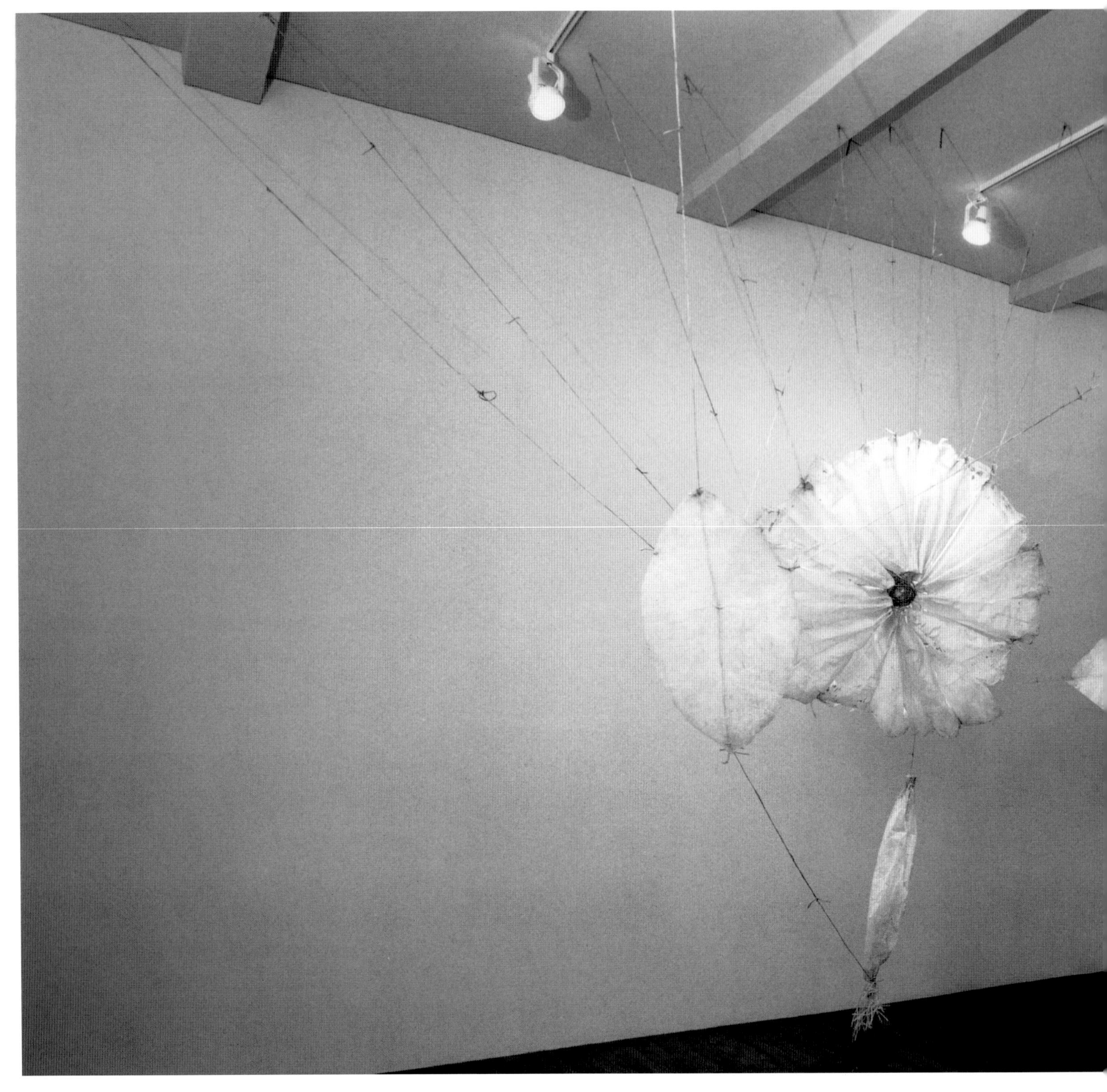

"A Flower for Ethyl Eichelberger" was my first transparent tape piece. Ethyl Eichelberger and his circle stylistically influenced how I think and feel about my video sets and costumes. — Minimal means for maximum impact.

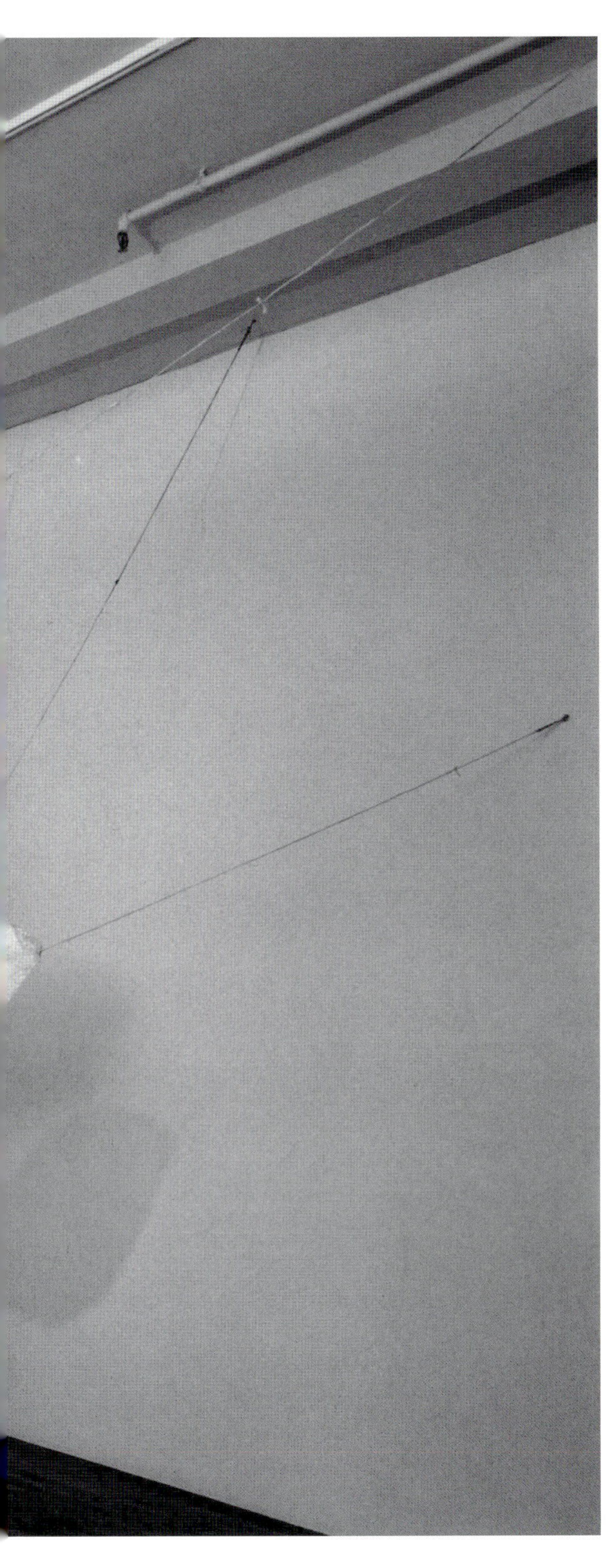

Like the flower, the jungle in
"Exit" (1999-2000), took about
two days to make. It depicts
a cardboard jungle and is
one of my favorite moments.
Miek is camouflaged against
a vine and will reveal himself
in a few shots later by lifting
his head.

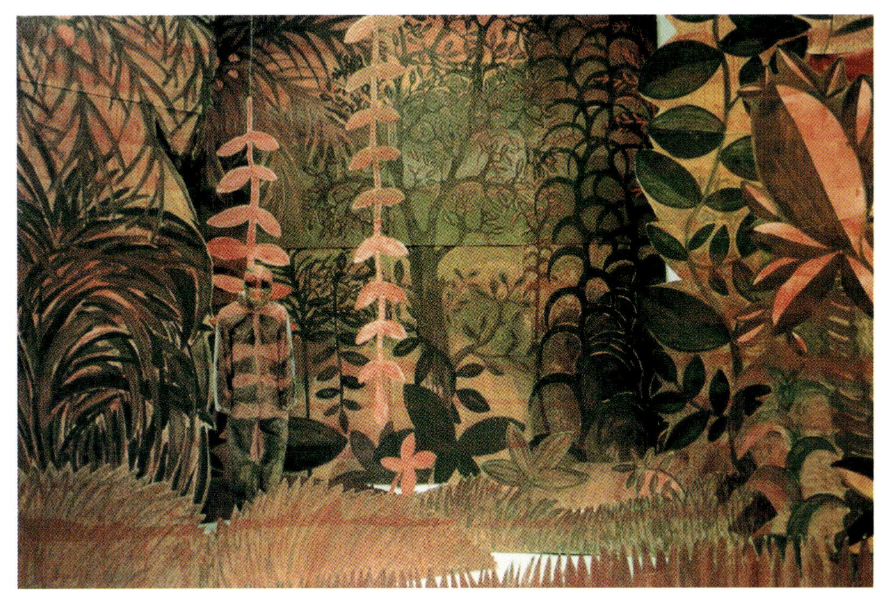

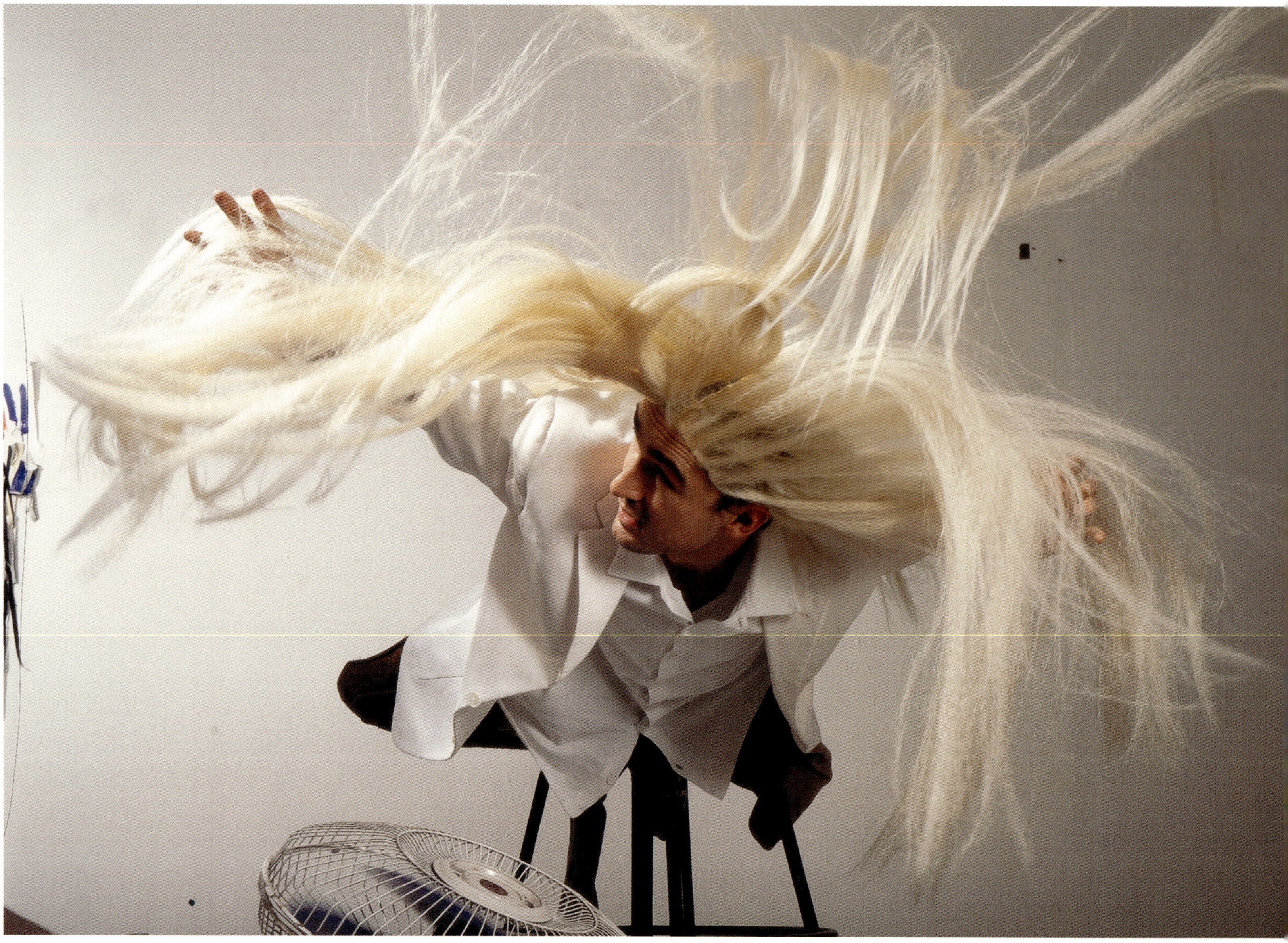

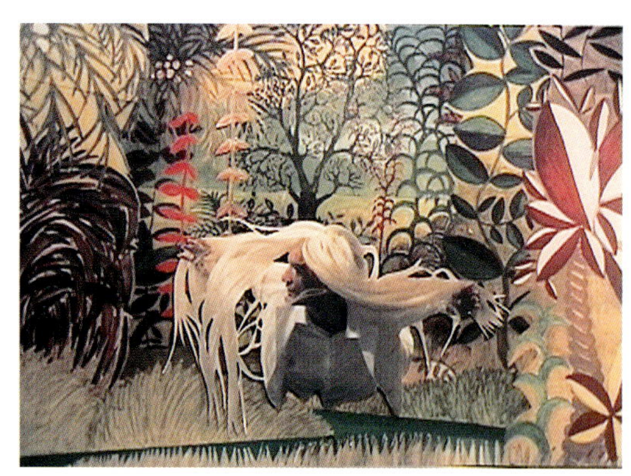

This is how low-teck I get. I wanted to fly in "Exit", so I simulated flying in part, with the movement of a lot of hair. First I photographed the jungle, then I photographed myself with two fans underneath my wig. After that I cut out the images that worked and placed their silhouette on top of the jungle. And finally I reshot them with my camera one image at a time.

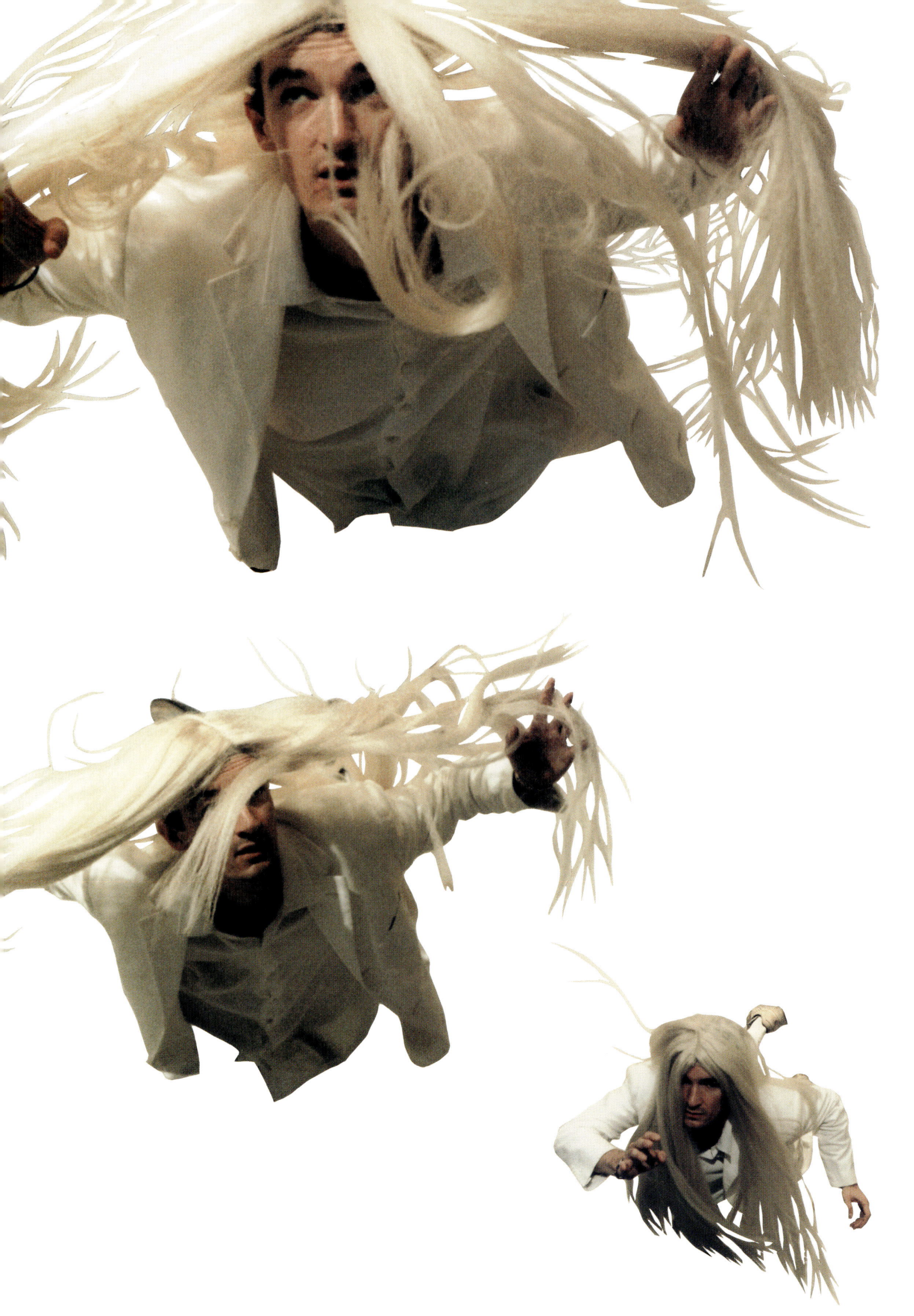

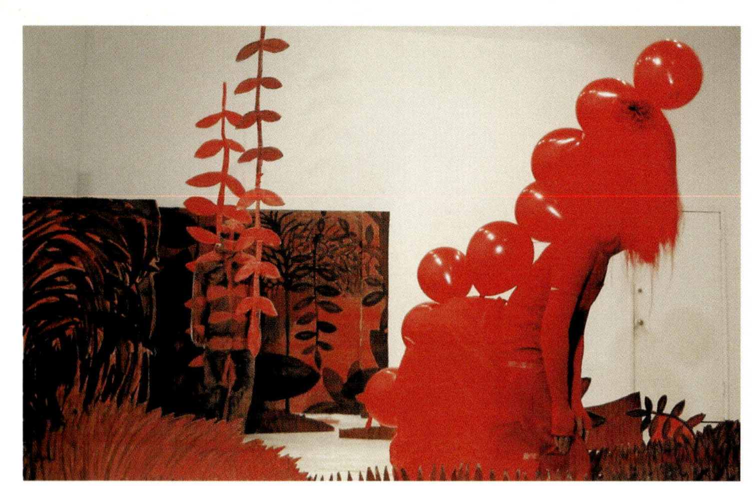

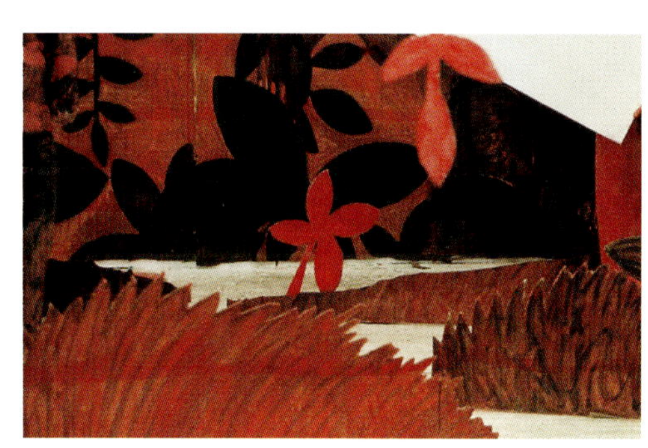

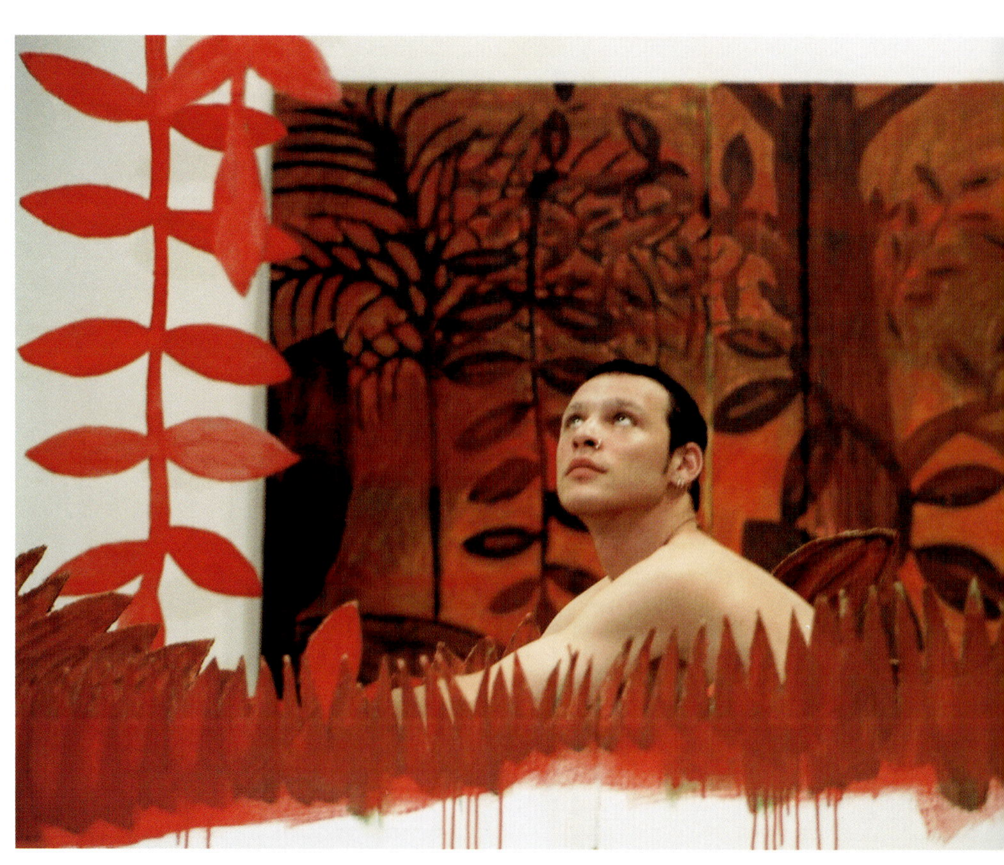

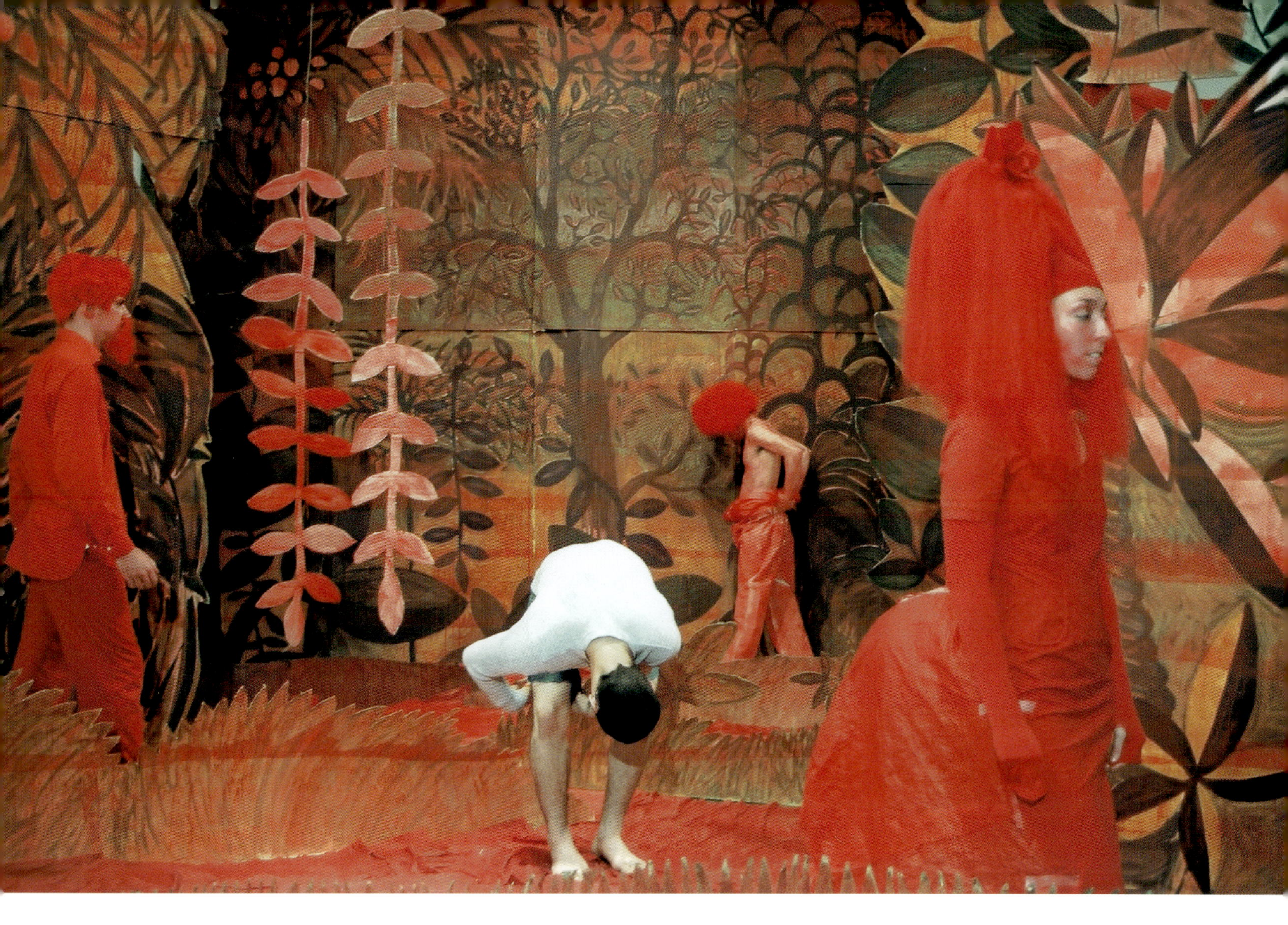

In the sequence above Miek is cutting off his clothing 1-2 inches at a time. The sequence took hours during which Matthew, Caroline and Filip couldn't move at all.

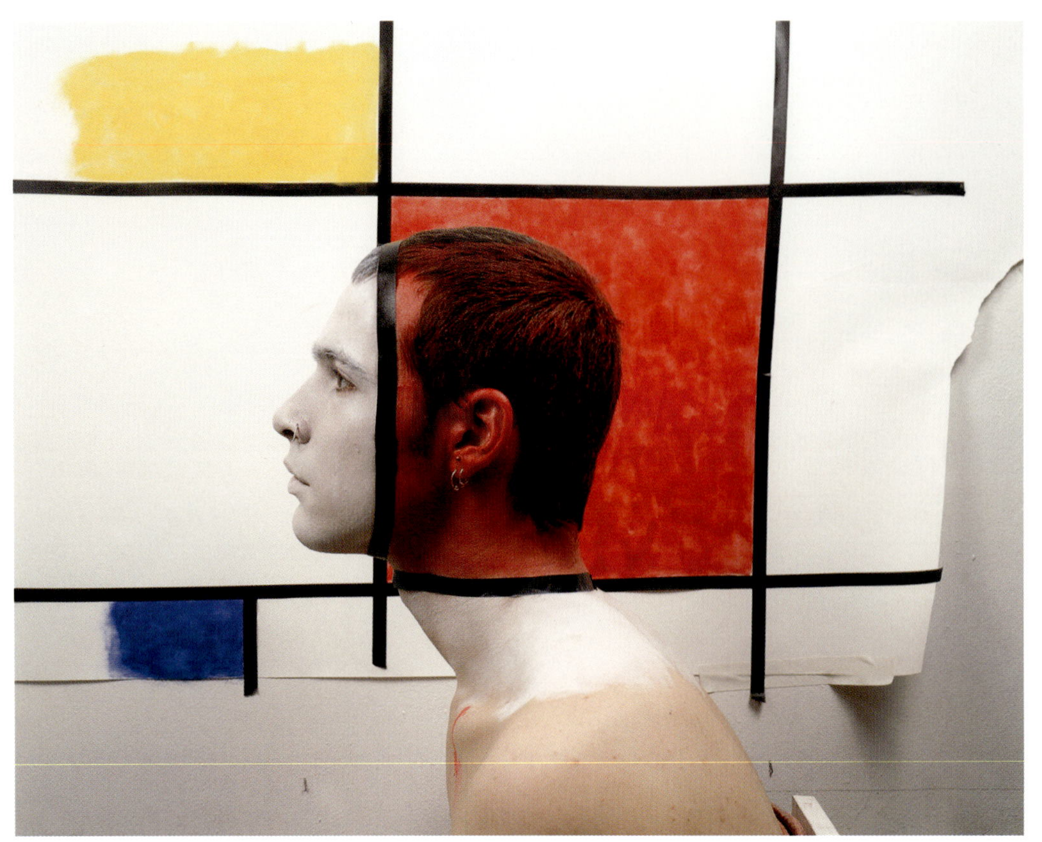

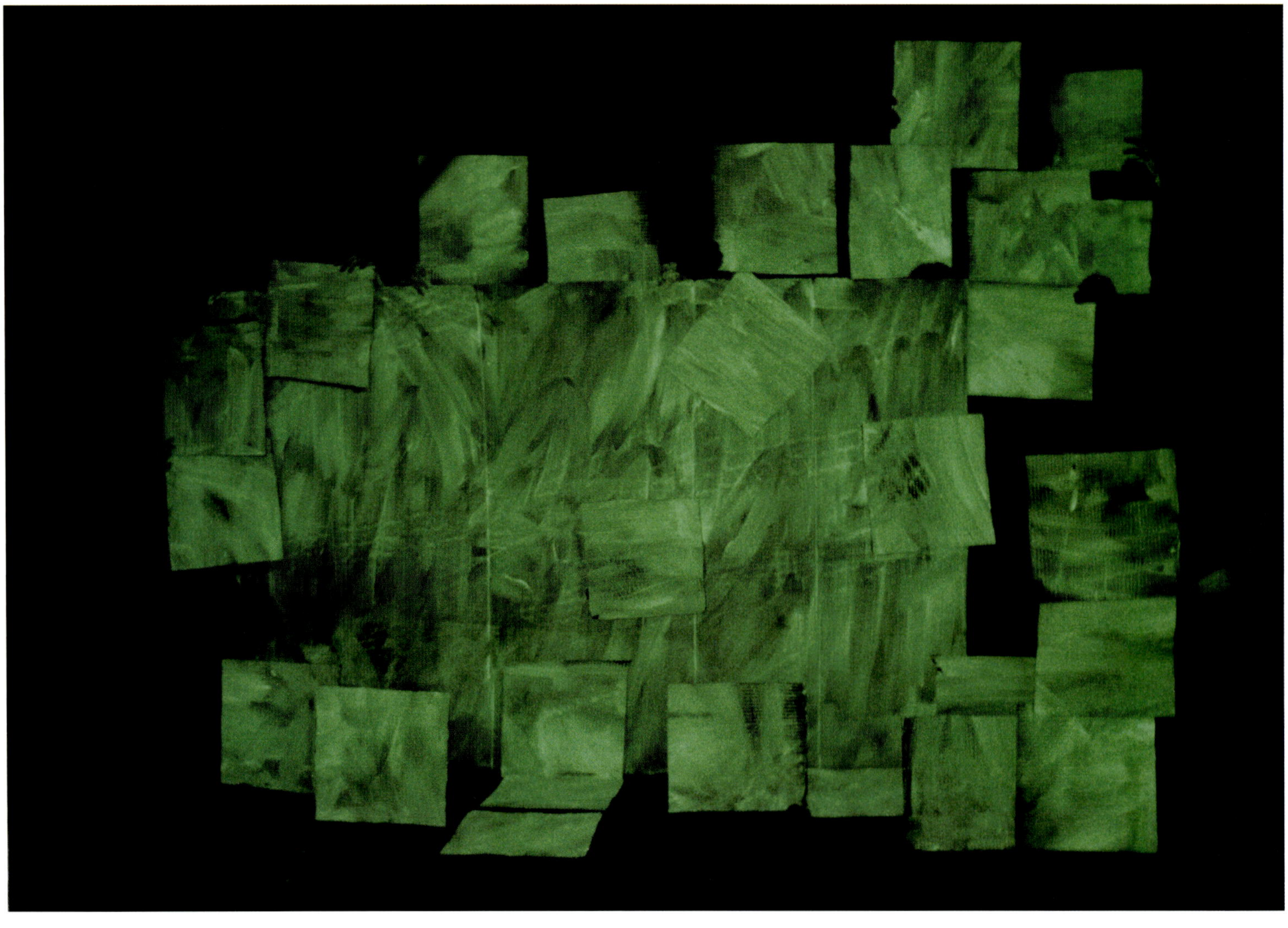

Influenced by the image as it appears on my video screen,
in many videos I treated the images as a row of
two-dimensional still-lifes. That often led me to deal
with them as paintings.

This is Mick in a scene from "The Sum and its Parts".
It is extracted from a sequence in which I painted
← Mondrian-esque patterns onto his face that shifted
around from take to take. The sequence, while only
a minute or two, took two weekends to film.

In this image from "Little Dances of Misfortunes", I
used phosphorescent paint, (mostly on my actors), but
↙ here on cardboard sheets arranged into ever changing
sculptures, or paintings.

"Two One Day Shetches".

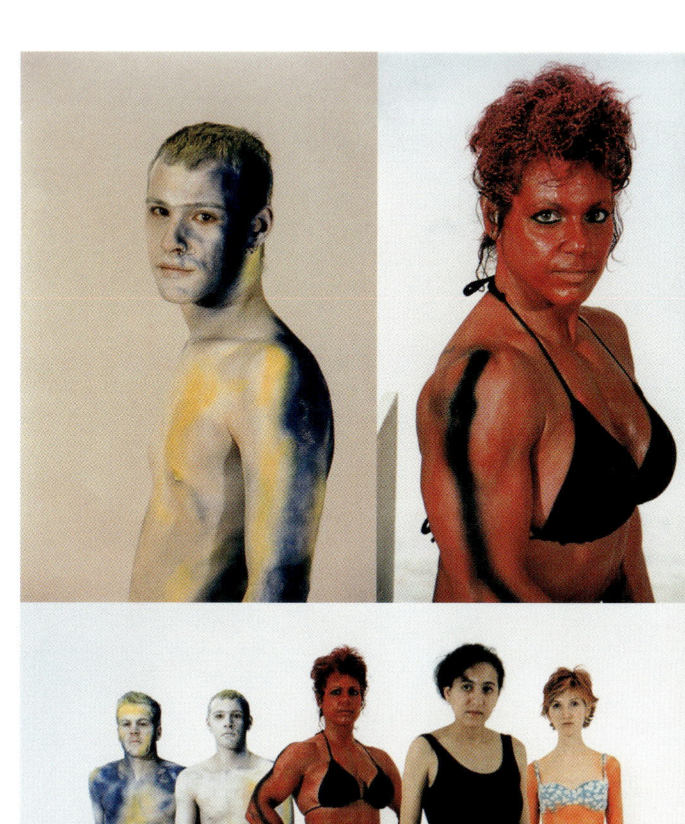

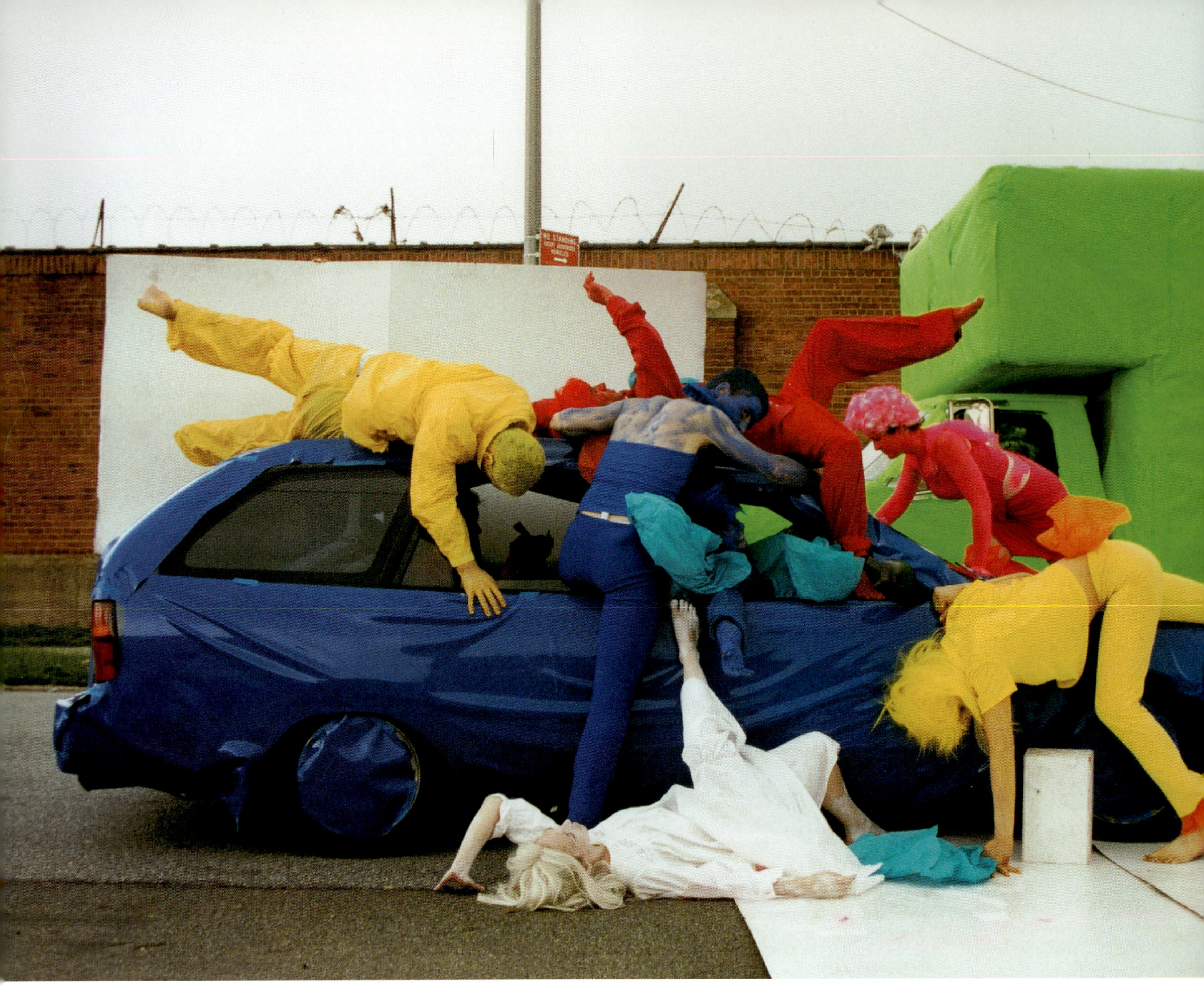

In some scenes I emphasize sculpture by placing props and performers into what I think of as quintessentially sculptural situations, — on pedestals. These moments are endpoints that are achieved through a series of performancelike situations in which I either strip down a set or accumulate a set until it reaches a certain climactic complexity. When I include more traditional expectations and clichés for sculpture in my videos, I subvert them, or integrate them into a layer and more diverse, sometimes personal context.

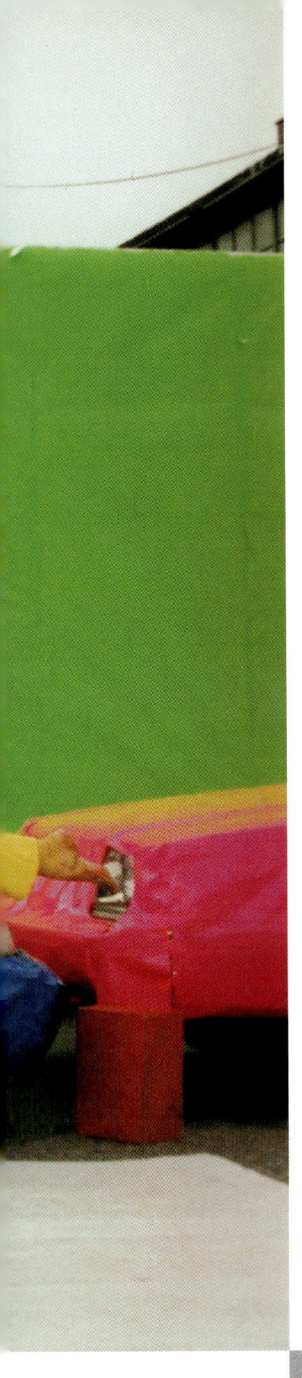

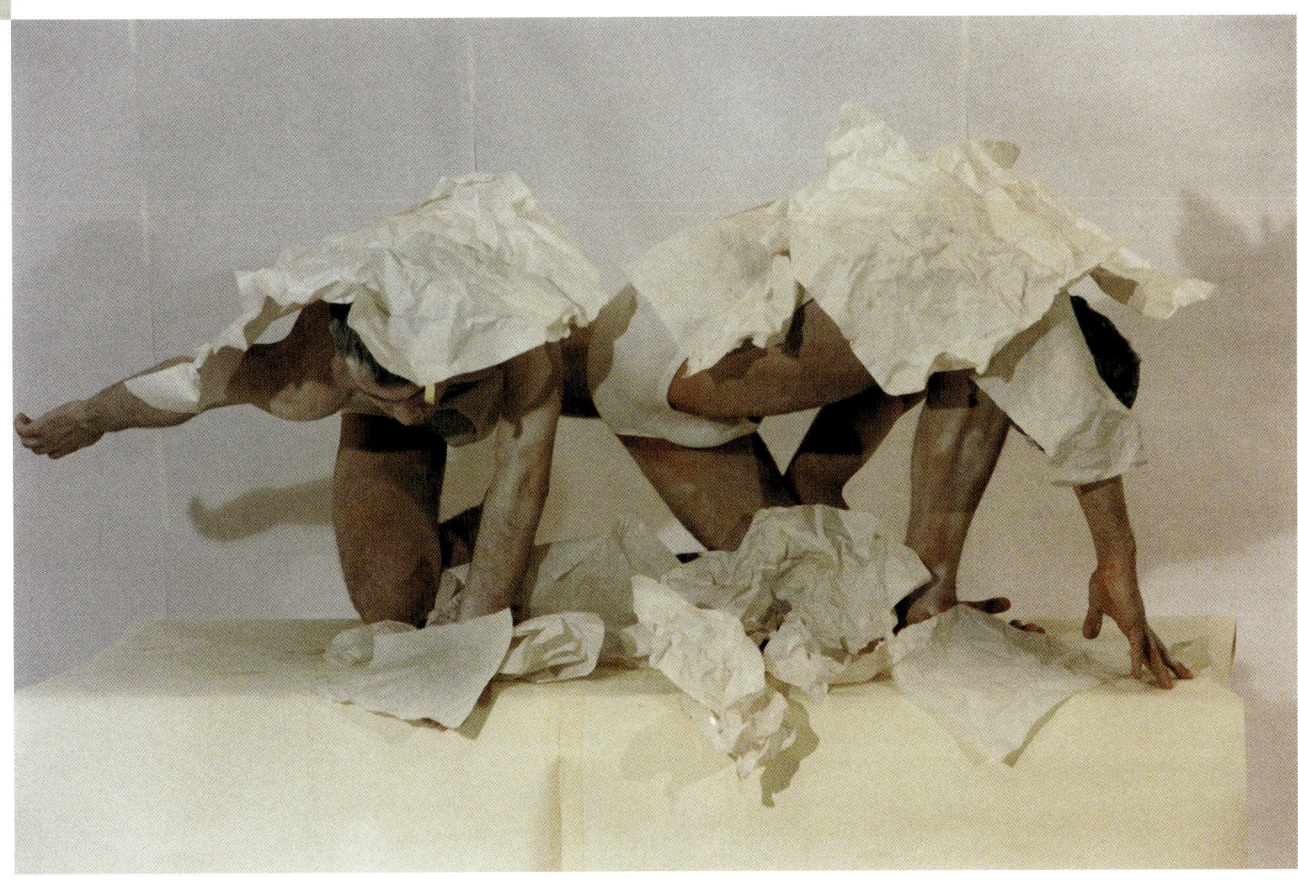

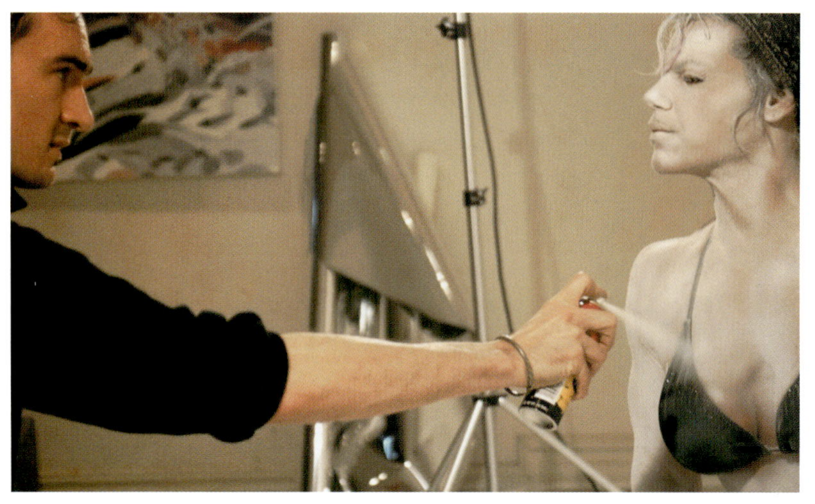

In "Two One Day Sketches", a professional bodybuilder, Fran Ferraro, is painted in horizontal 3-4 inch stripes from her feet to her head. In this photo I freshen-up the white which had started to run in the unbearable heat of the studio that day.

Same video, a little later. Fran's look has turned into what I see as the combination of a powerhouse Amazone with a heart of gold and a Franz West sculpture.
↙

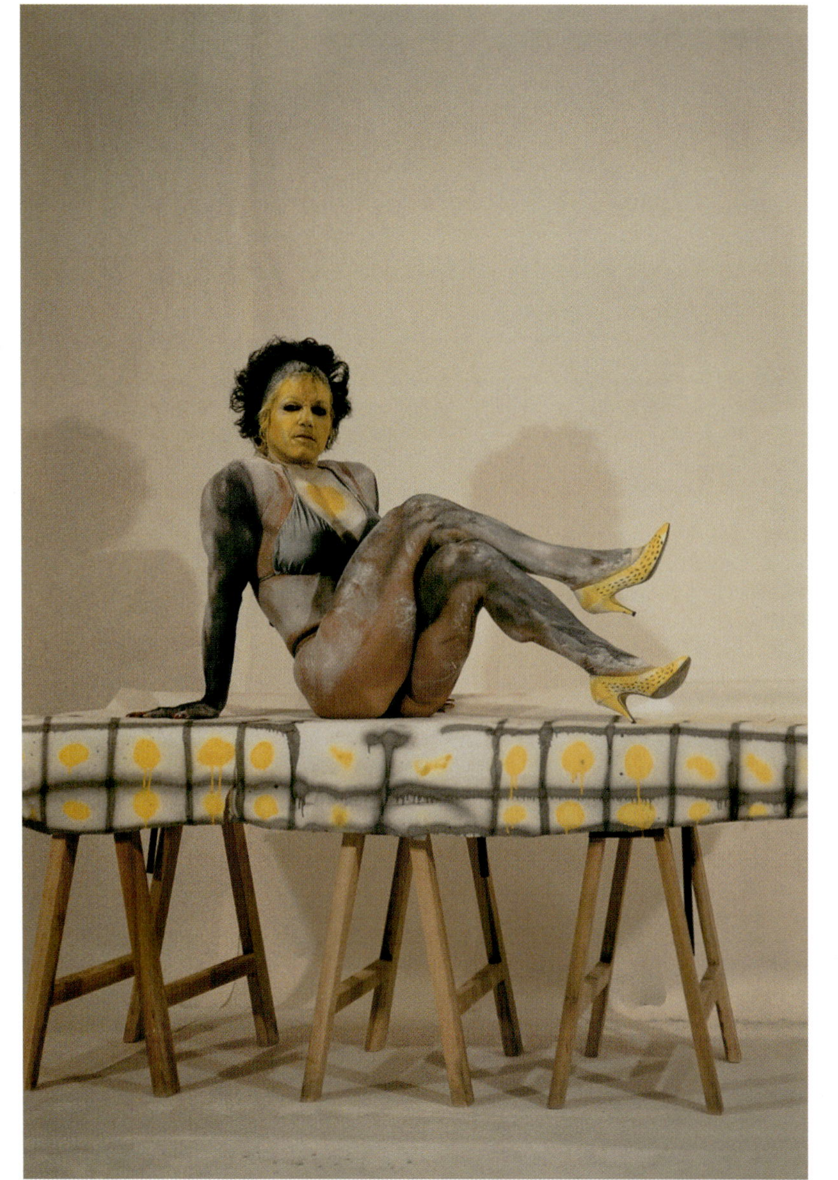

This is an image from "Sketch for Little Dances of Misfortunes", I made using phosphorescent paint. Whenever I turned the light off, Mick's body would retain some light for a split second. Put together the sequence created the effect of a pulse. The photo nicely captures that moment.
→

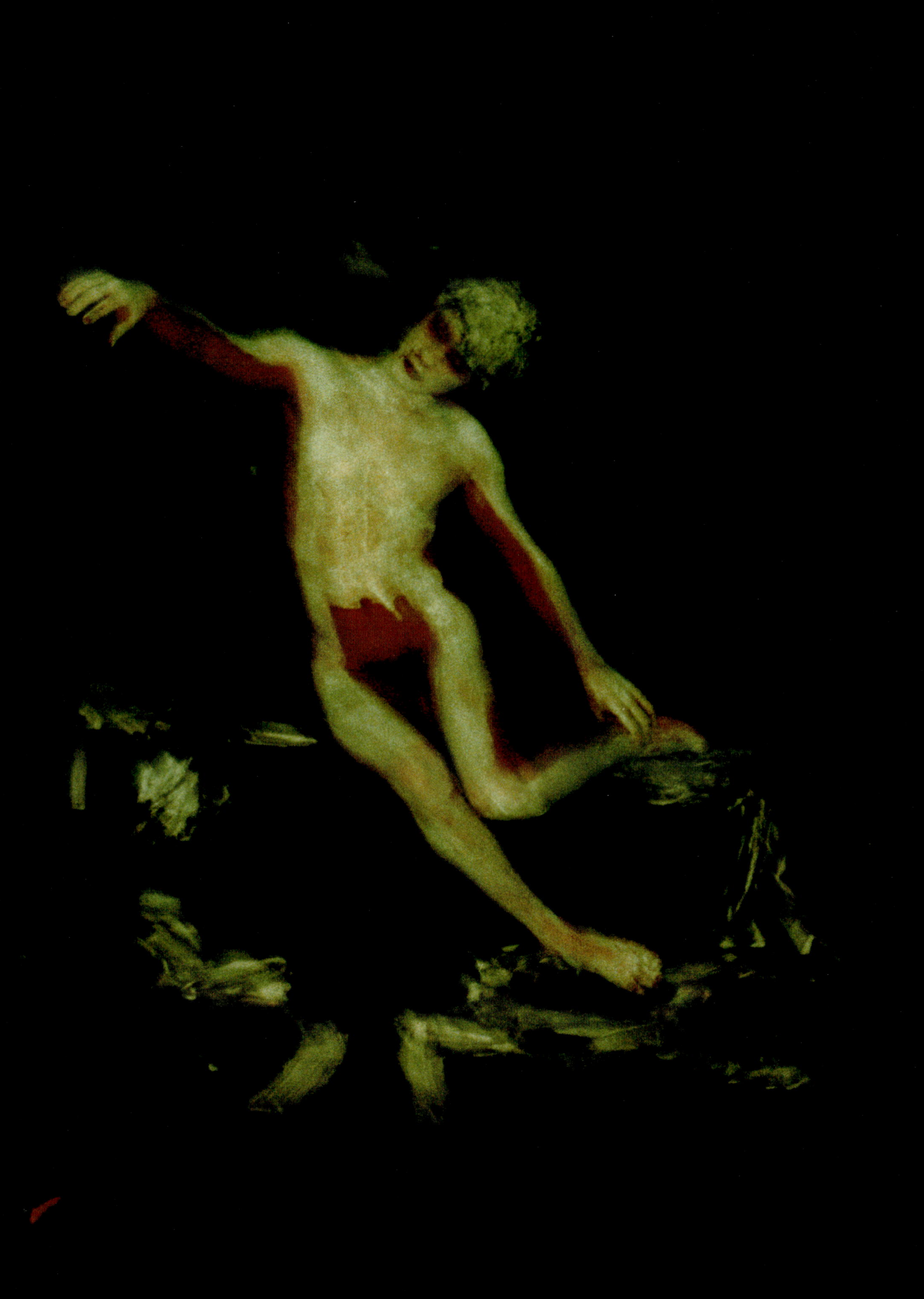

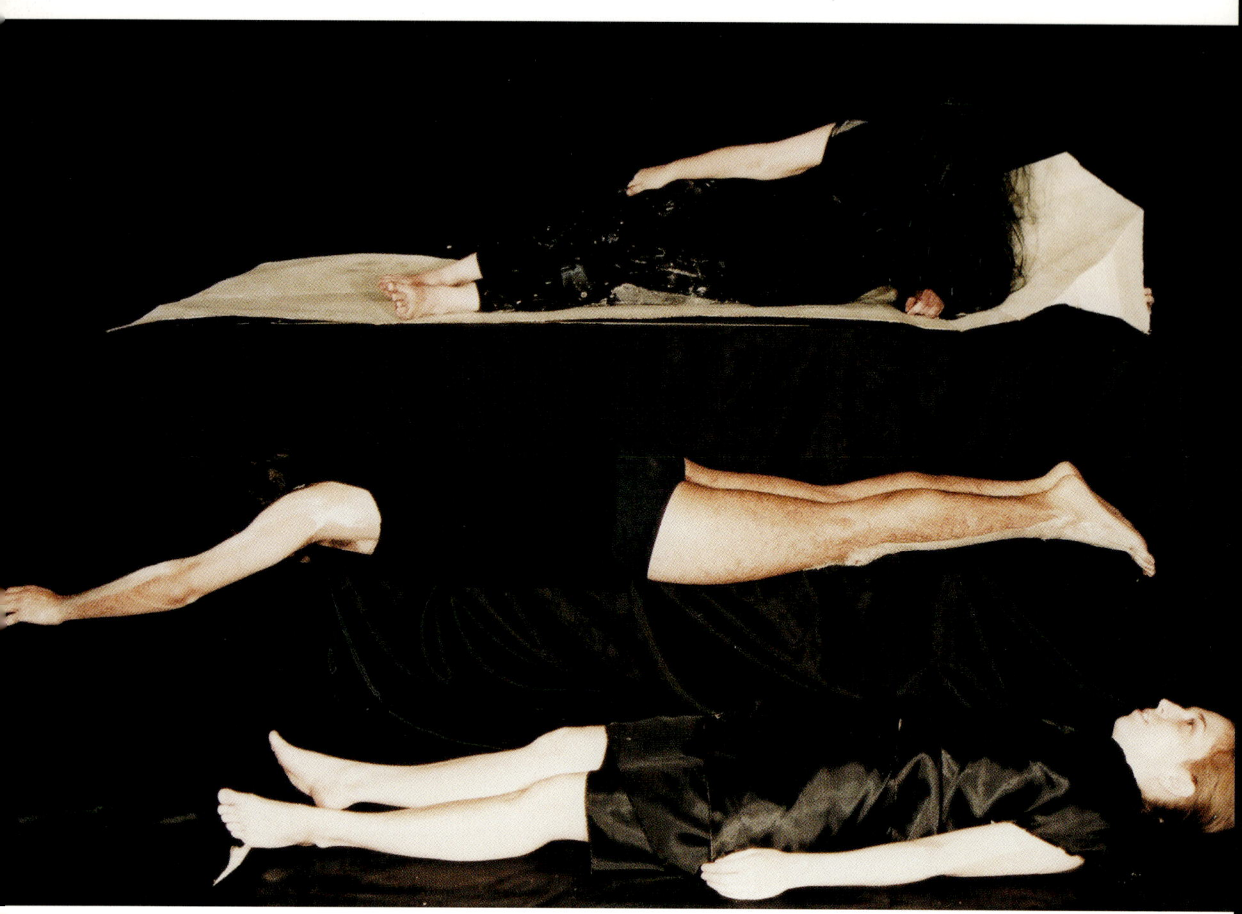

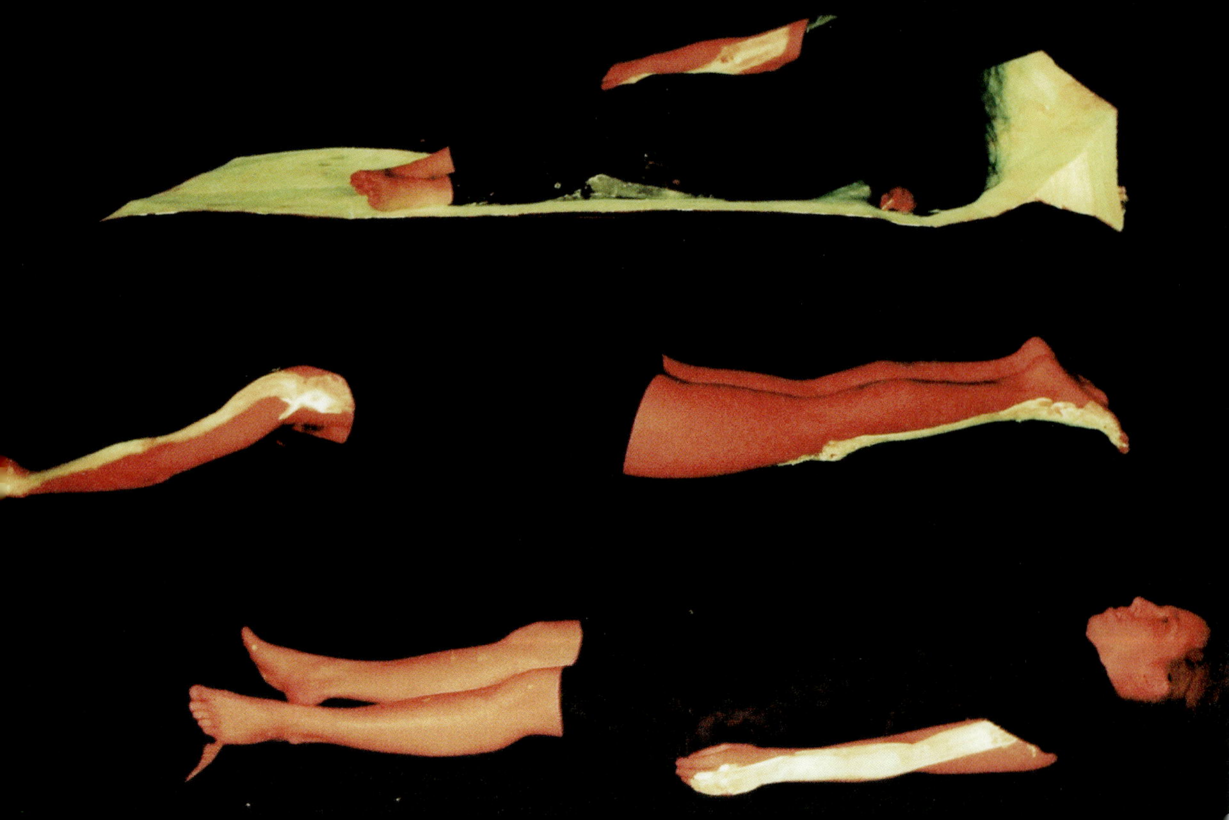

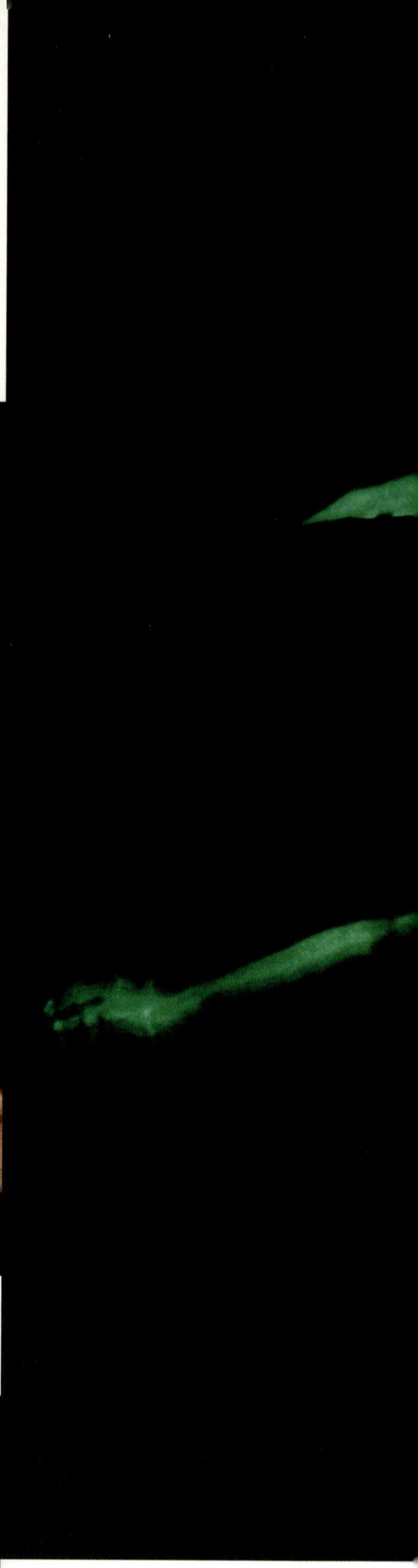

This is one of those perfect, transitional sculpture on pedestal moments from "Little Dances of Misfortunes" that lasted for one shot only. Caroline (bottom) incrementally moved from left to right, Javier (center) moved from right to left and Joyce stayed put. In the video they float horizontally cutting the space into three planes.

In some of my knit pieces from around the time I started
to use the camera, I pushed for a sense of inherent motion. I
would, for instance, challenge myself to start knitting in one corner
of the piece and literally move accross the surface of the armature
trying to avoid the use of seams in order to make the piece seem
to flow.
This created currents and crosscurrents on the surface which were
further accentuated by the reflected light on the knit silver
mylar's broken surface.

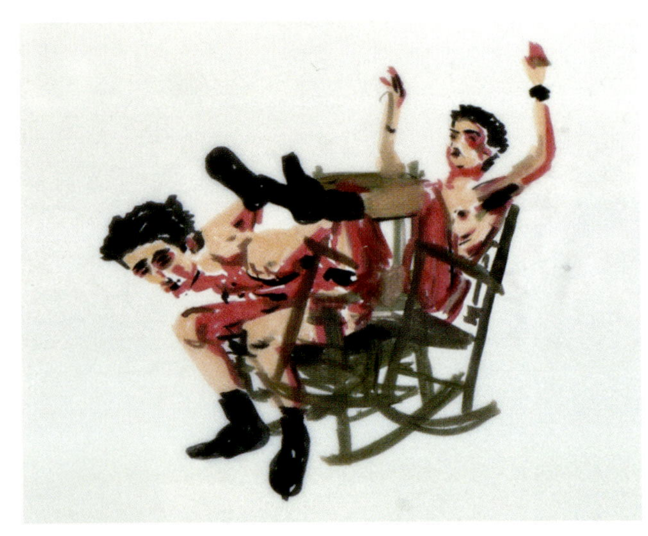

For "Double Rocker" I filmed myself in a rocking chair
moving forewards and backwards. Then I replayed the
footage on TV, froze individual images and traced them
over each other. From one of those drawings I built
a wire structure and finally knit along the armature.

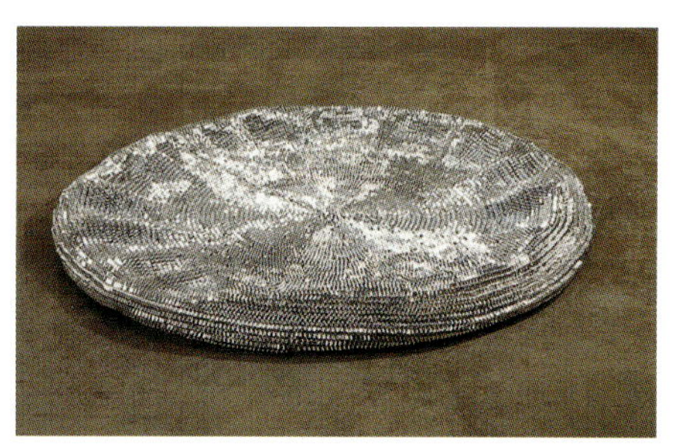

For "Distorted Round #1 and 2", circularity seemed to express an inevitability and never-ending motion to the process and pieces.

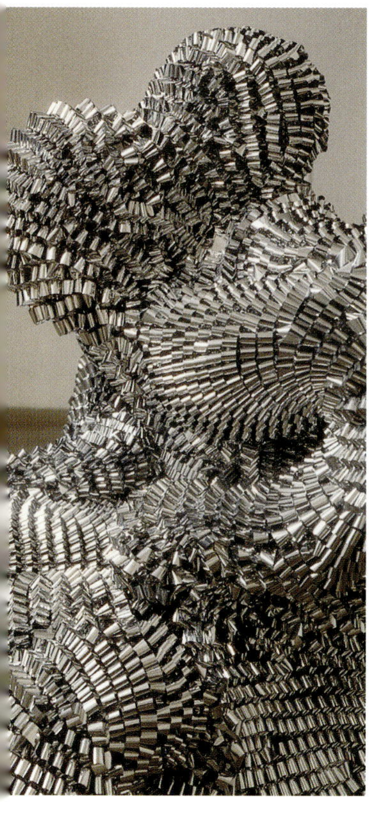

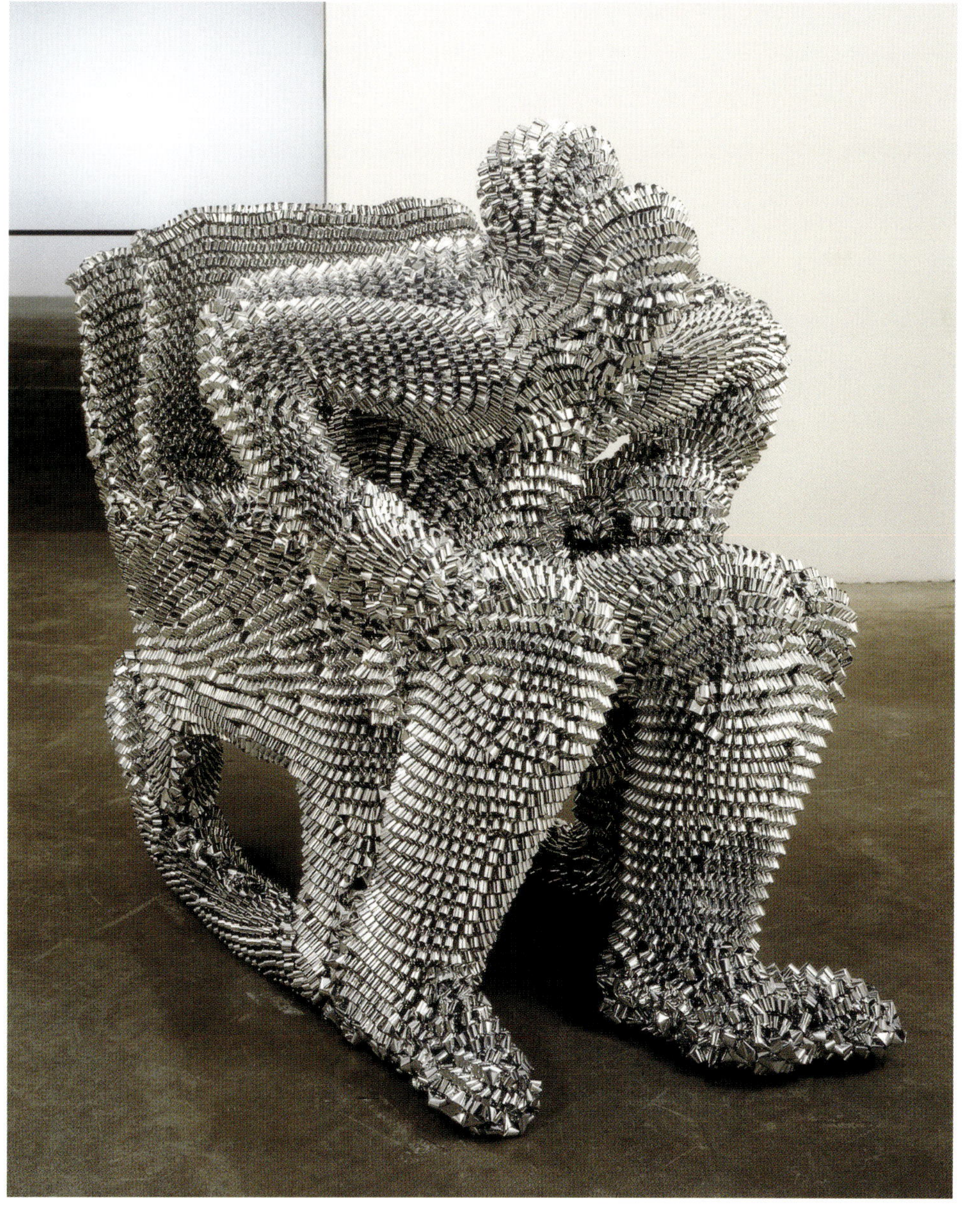

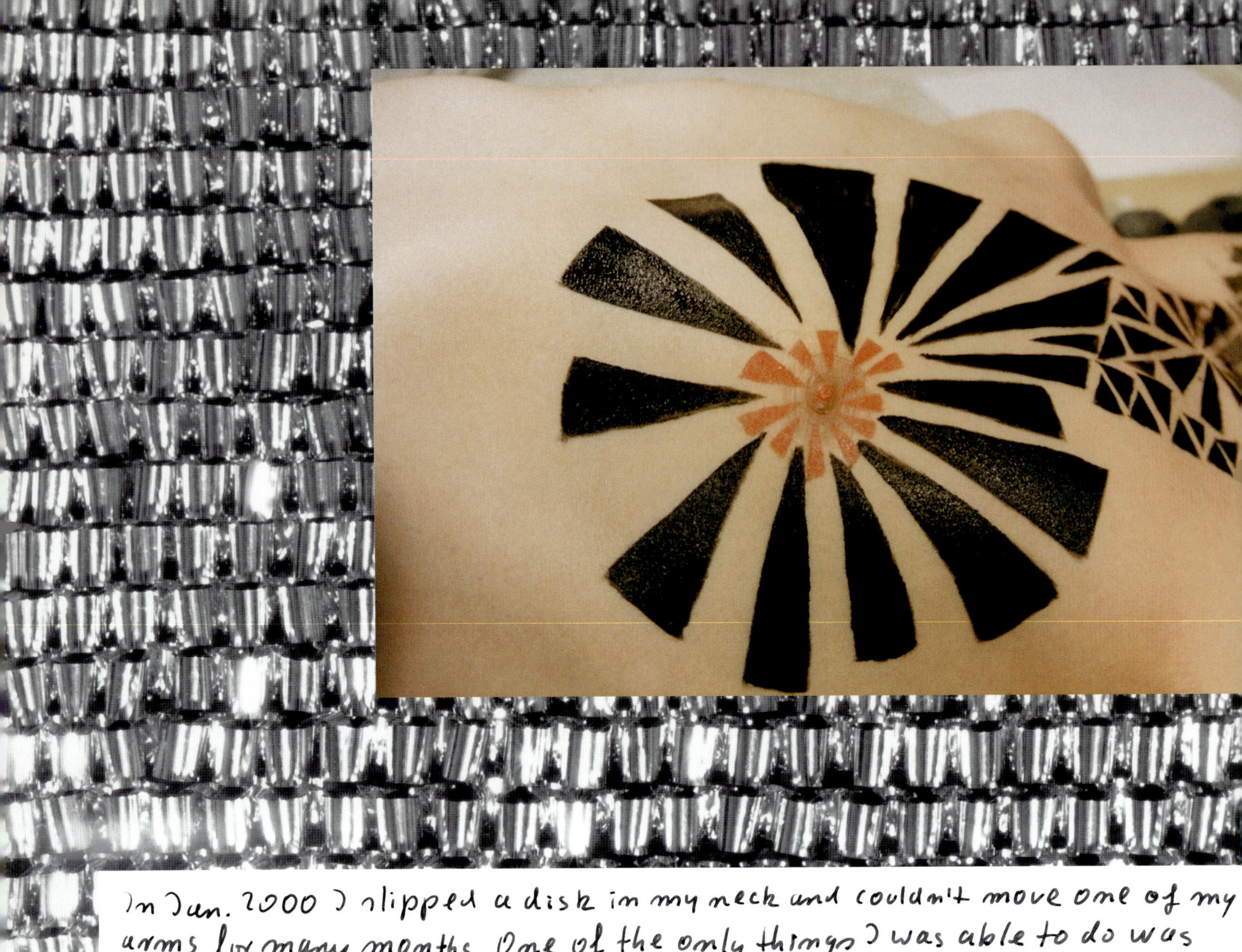

In Jan. 2000 I slipped a disk in my neck and couldn't move one of my arms for many months. One of the only things I was able to do was shoot videos on a relatively intimate scale. Mick and I met for 3-4 months just about every weekend and experimented. The collected experiments made up "The Sum and its Parts".

In most of my videos the sense of motion is experienced through transformation, but in this sequence, the final sequence from "The Sum and its Parts", I follow the marks that I painted onto Mick's body so closely with the camera that one doesn't have a sense of his body as an entirety until some time after one has traveled on it. This sequence is probably as close as any of my filmed sequences to the experience of knitting, which is mostly abstract and for me, about being absorbed in moments and detail.

Those photographs offer a different experience. In them one sees the body and gets a sense of the whole.

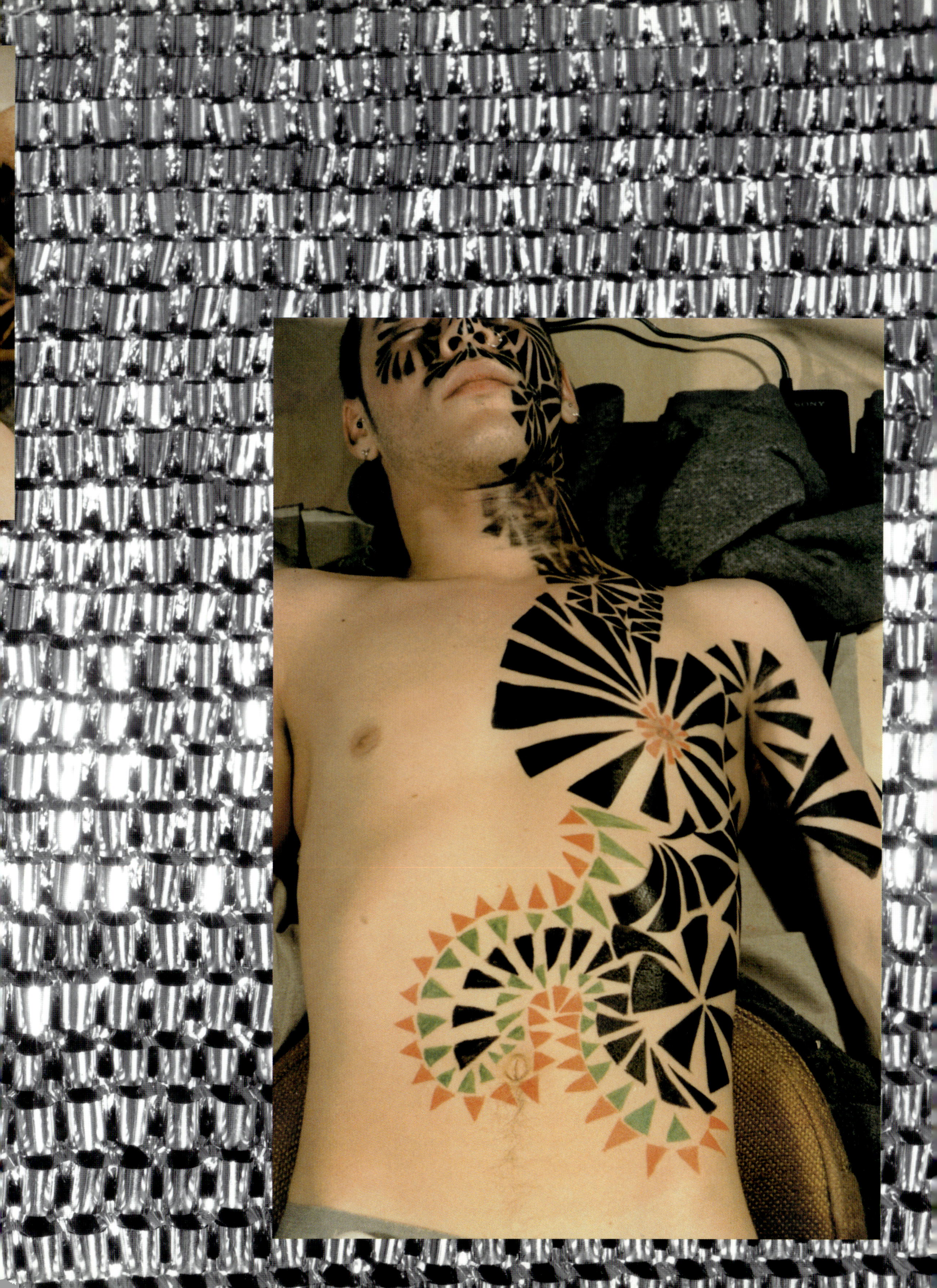

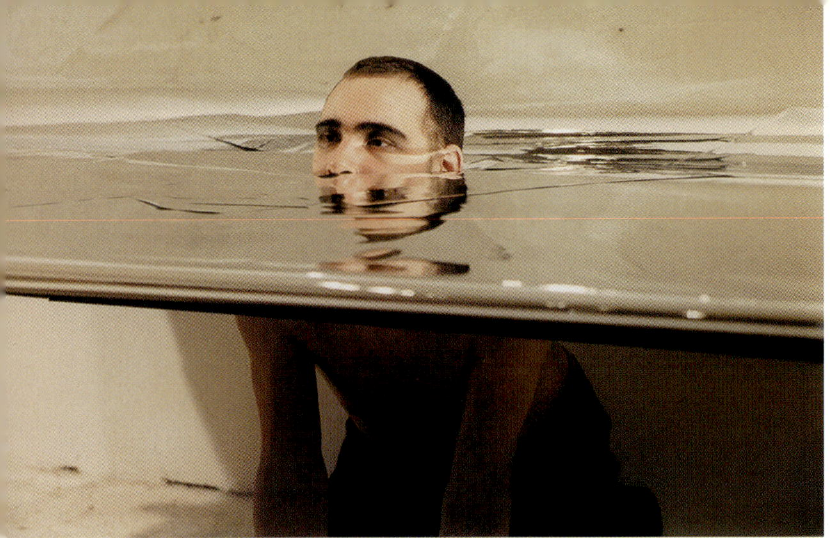

1.

The theme here is that there is no stable ground. Any surface has another surface below it. It was something I believed when I made my first work in response to Ethyl Eichelberger's death and it has continued to find its way into my work in many guises.

2.   3.

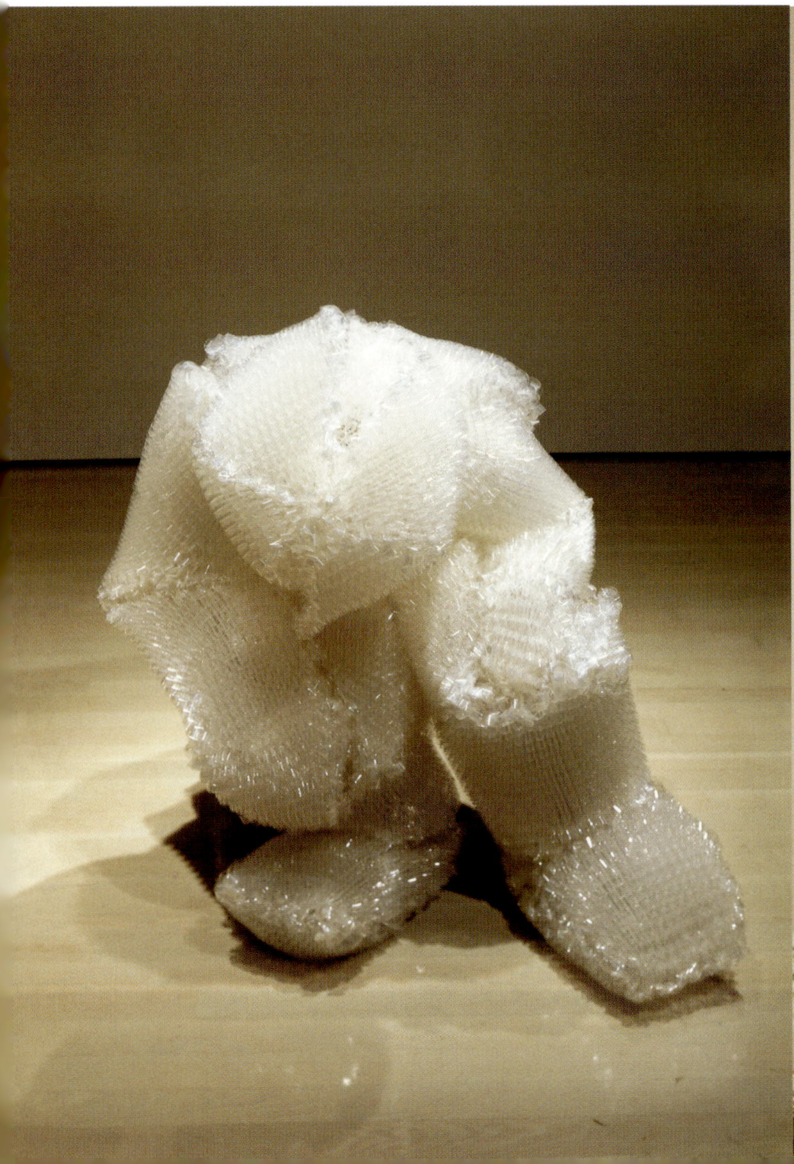

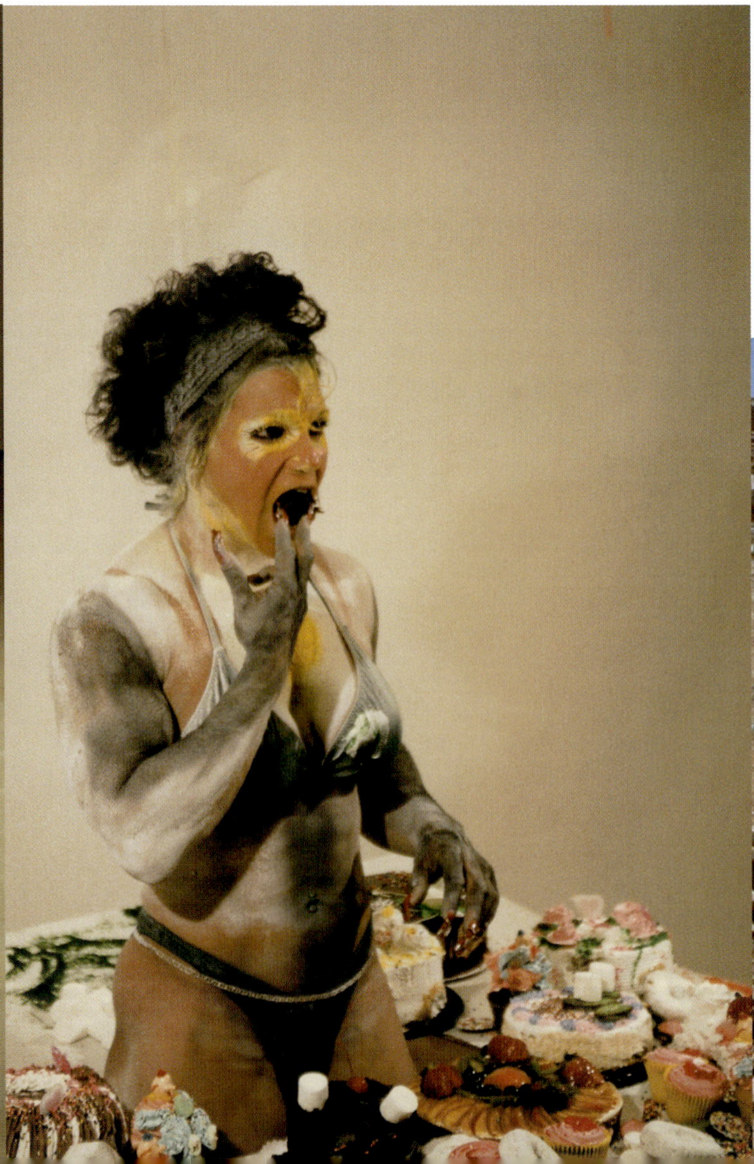

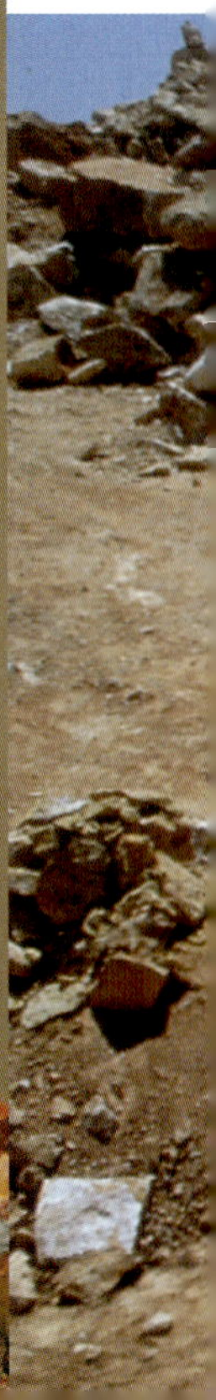

Mick in "The Sum and its Parts"

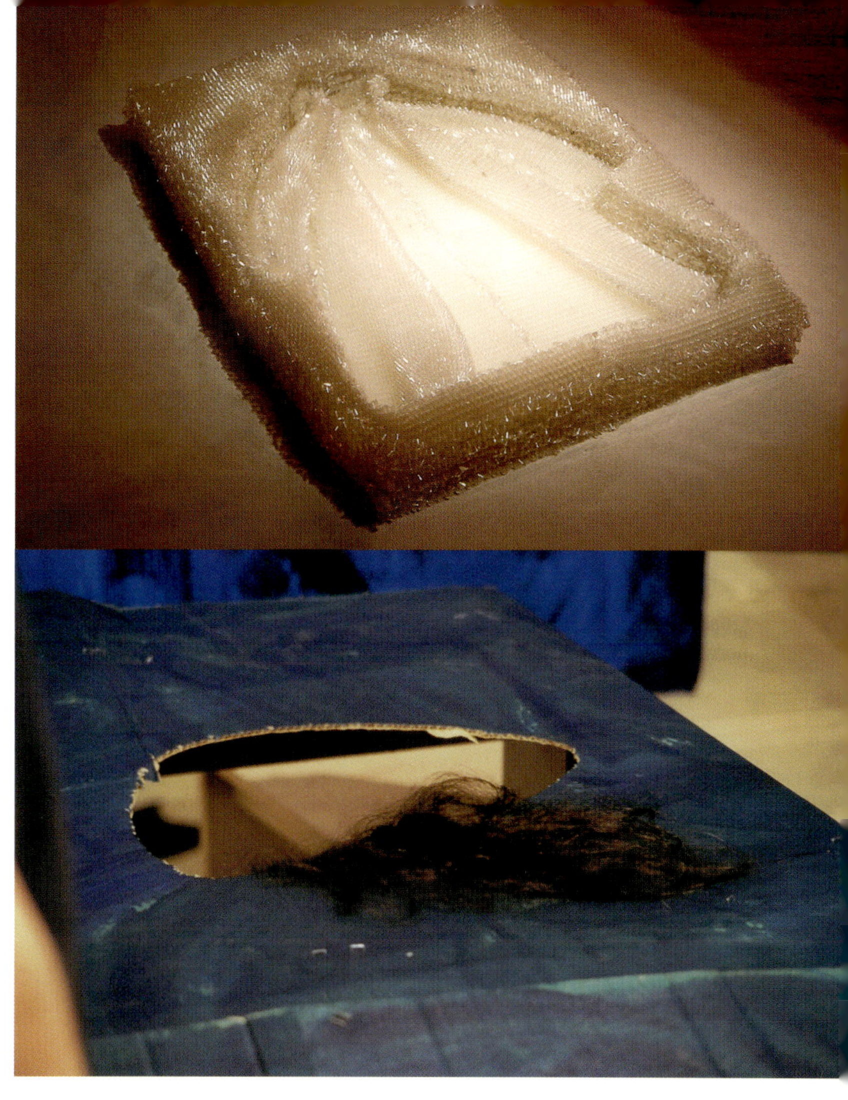

. "Multiple Fake" in which I layered
an armature modeled on a child
with five coats of knit surface,
obliterating most detail, then
excavating one arm back to the
second surface, (among other
excavations).

. Iran appearing out of the ground
and surrounded by lots of sweets.
("Two One Day Sketches").

4. "Framed by Darkness", — a
Performance in Israel's desert
in which I knit in a dug hole all day
and knit.

5. With "Fossil" a hole cut into a
wall was filled with what seemed
to be a floating figure.

6. Cecilia's hair just before it
disappears ("Sleepless Nights").

7. "Castle" in which a coat is
embedded in its own silhouette.

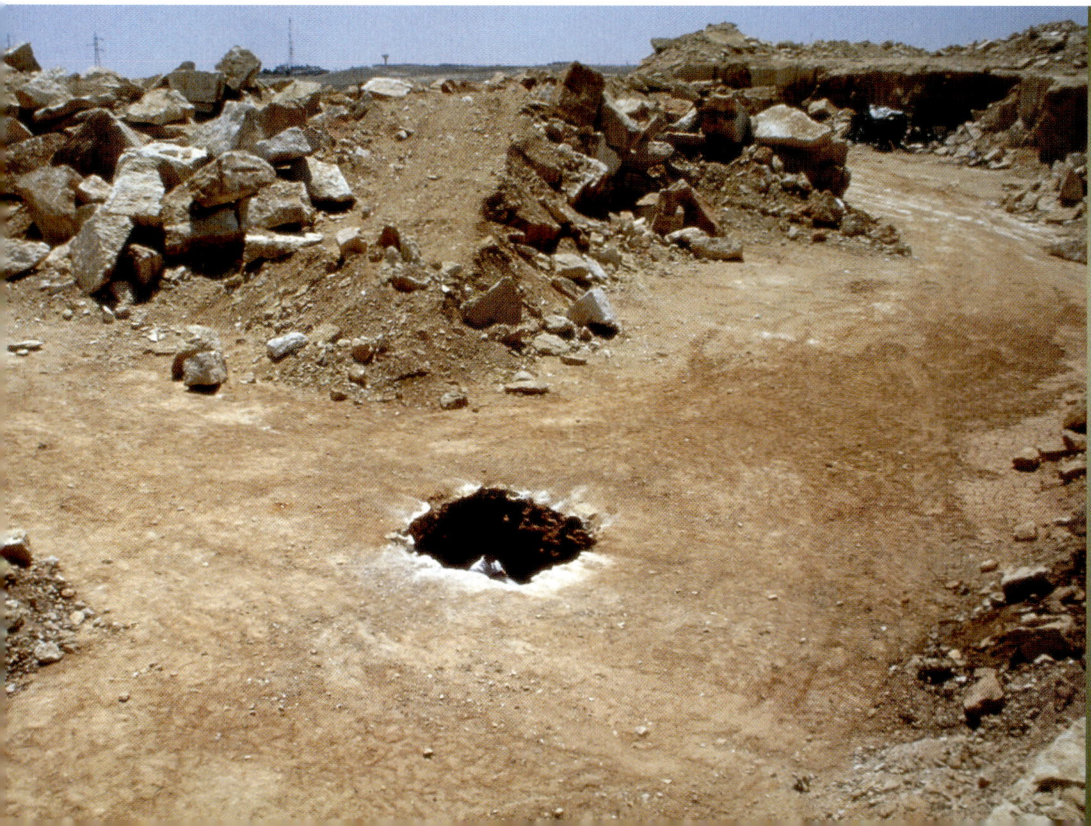

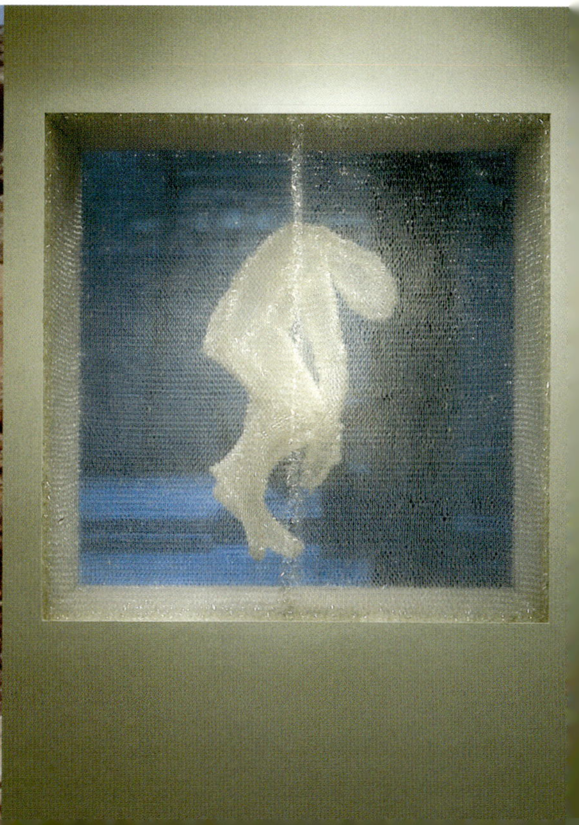

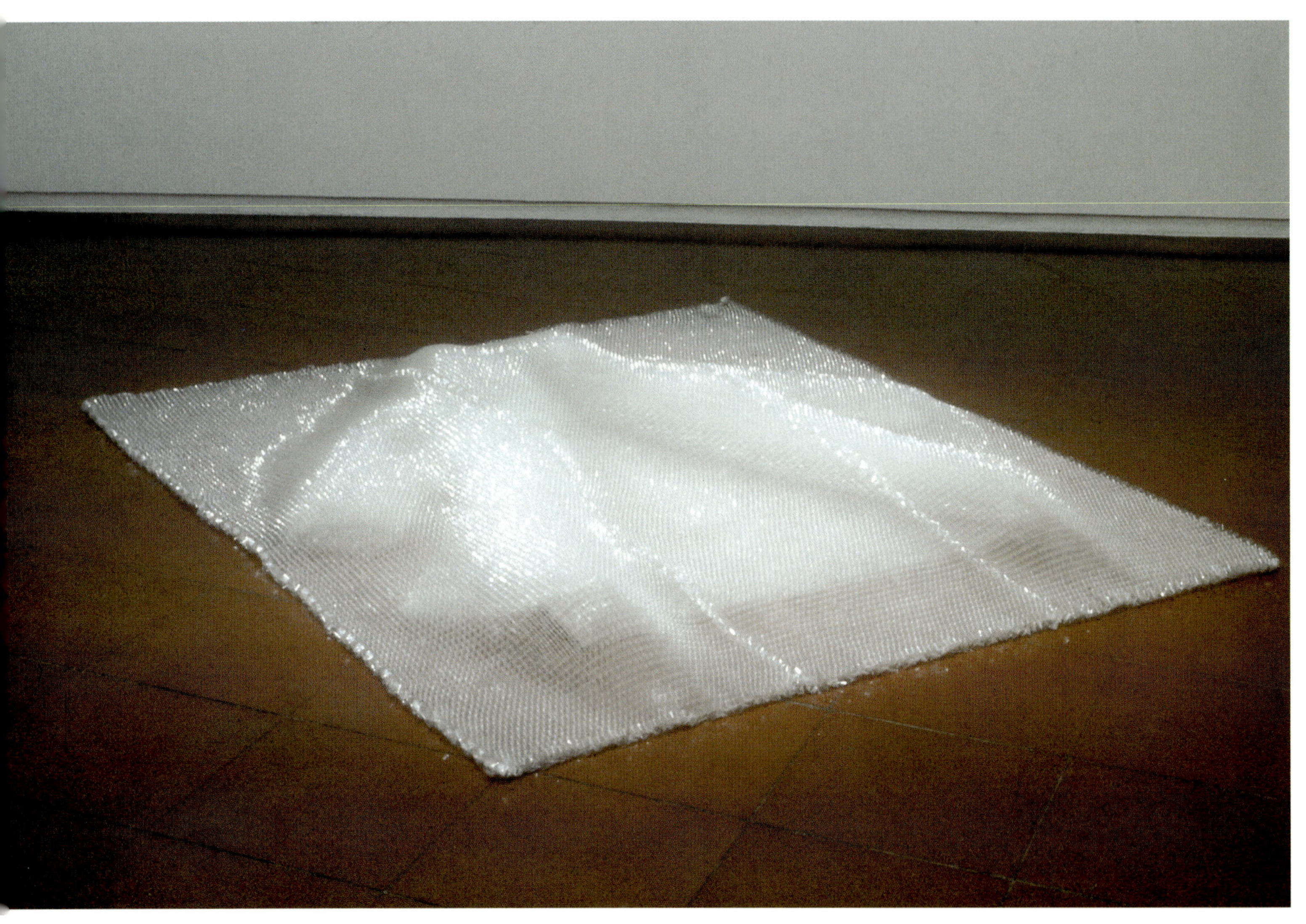

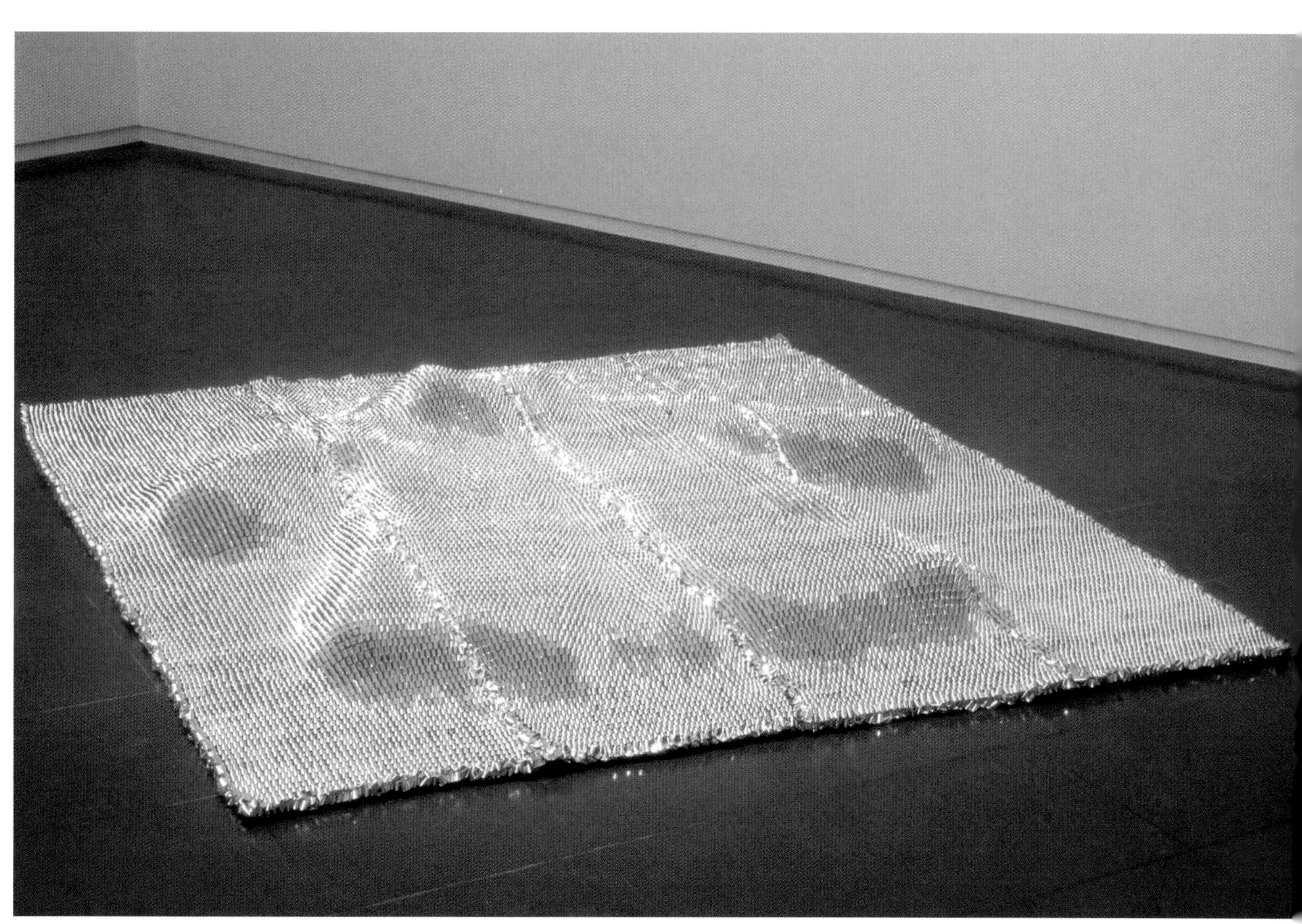

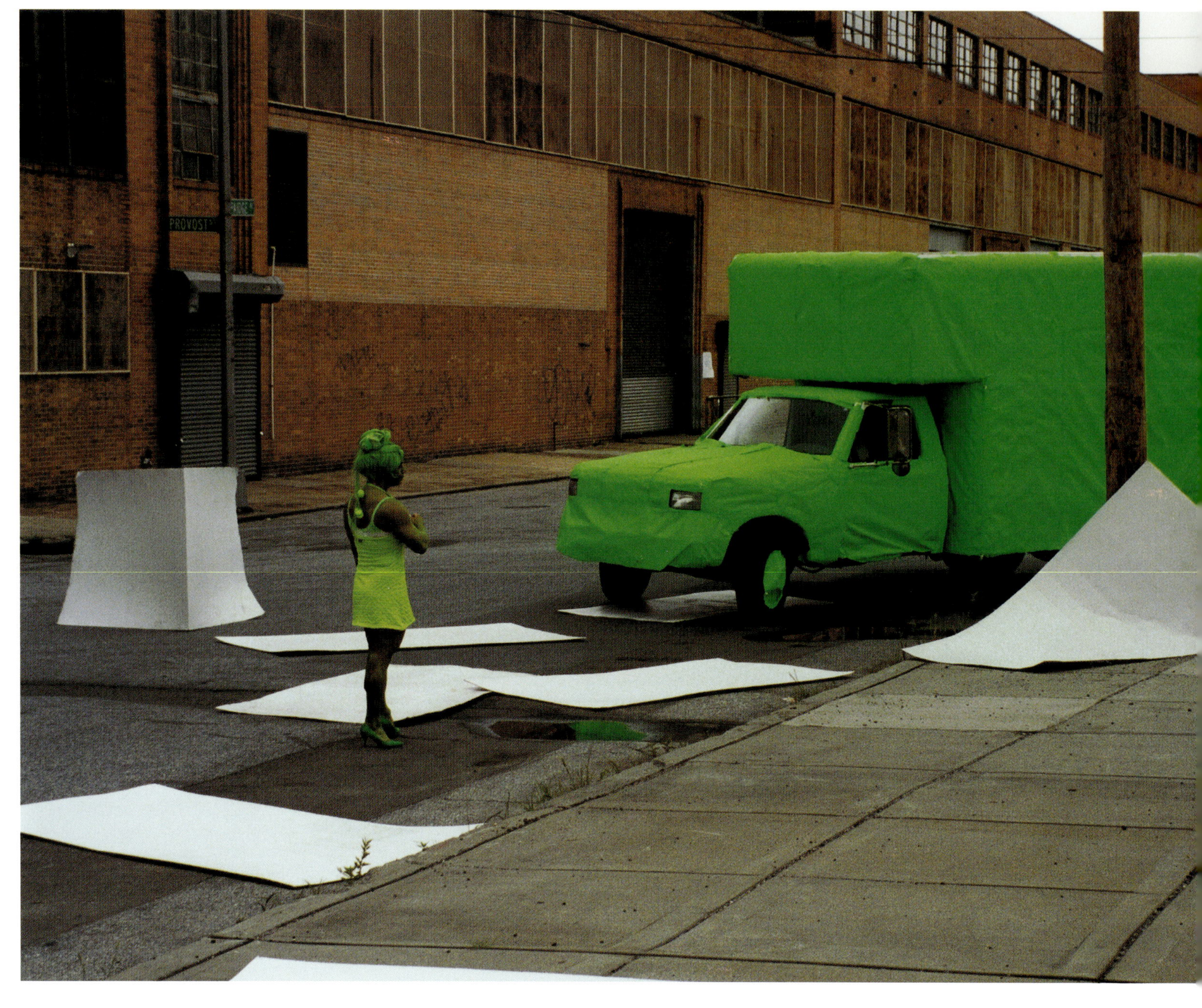

Green, blue, red..., the Chrysler Building -- "Pure Sublimation" had it all. There were firemen who let us use their toilets, five neighborhood kids who were easily persuaded to join in, and the next day's realization that, despite the rainy weather and heavy makeup, we all had sunburns.

In the red and pink sequence, Sascha did an acrobatic somersault over and across a car in increments.

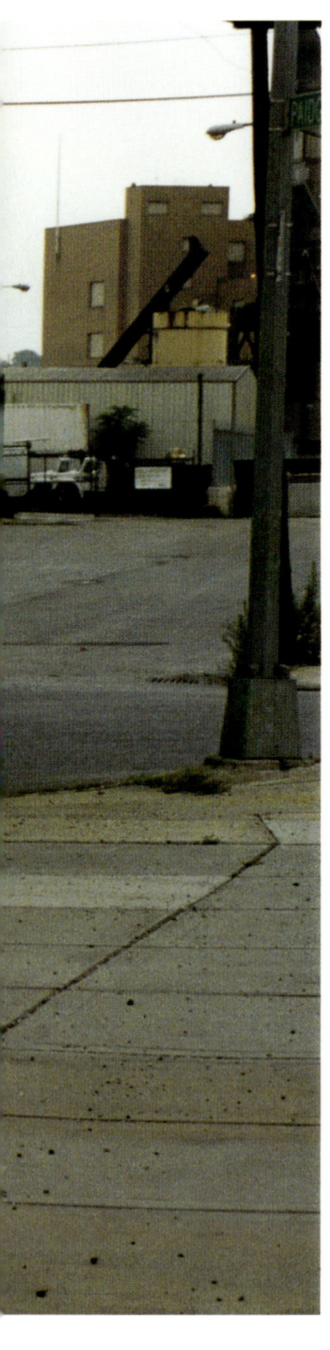

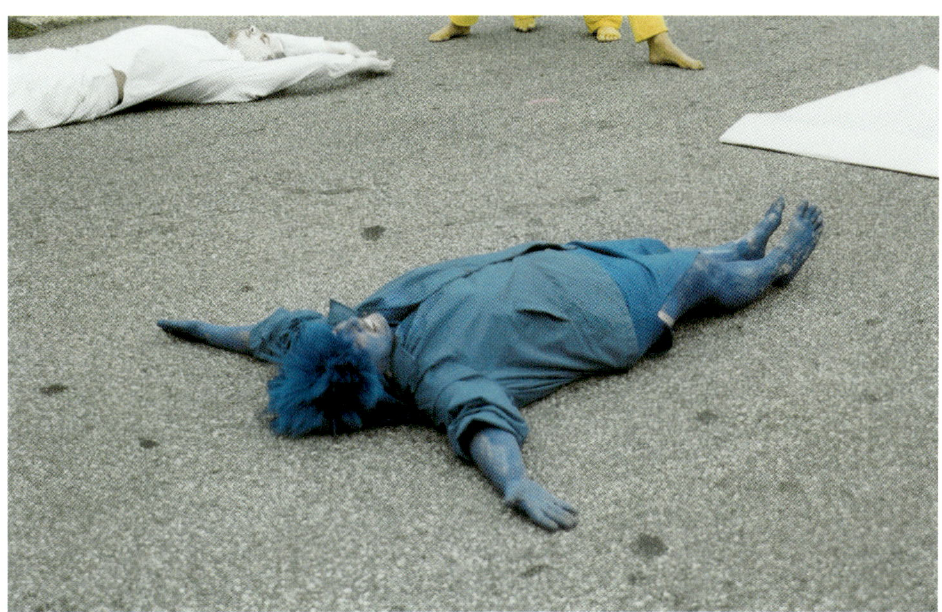

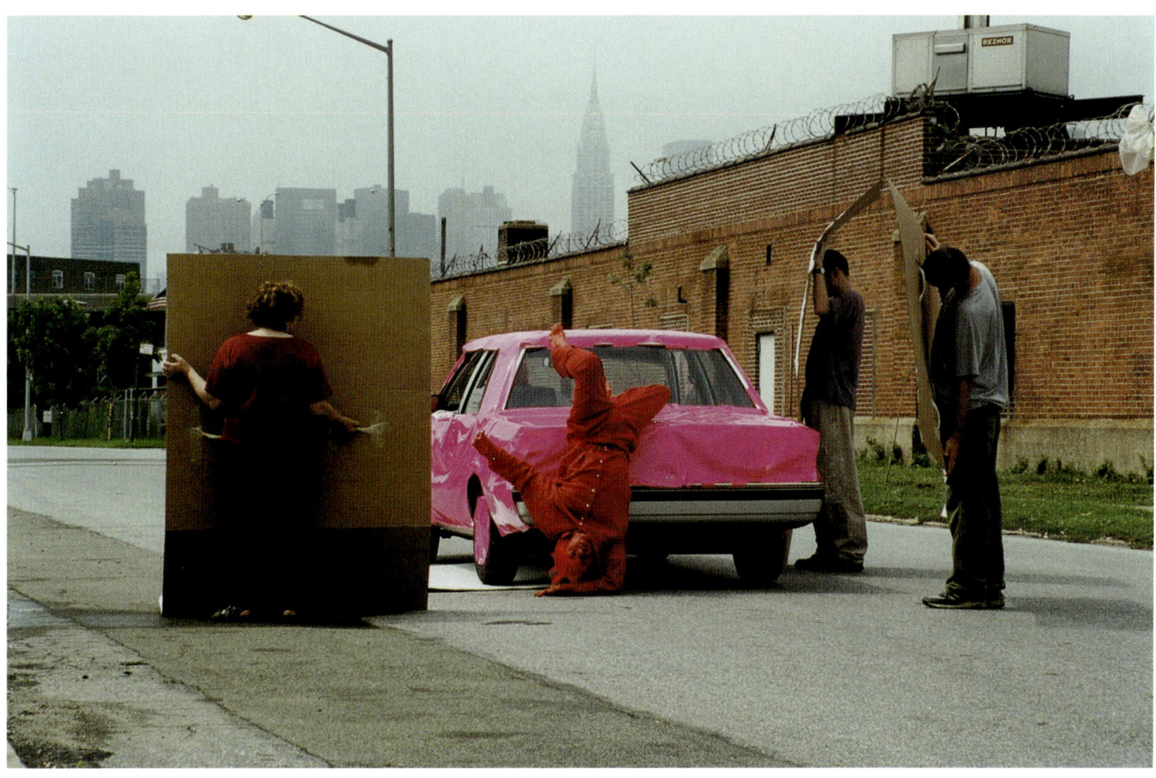

To emphasize the performance quality of both the videos and the photos, I have started to cut out some photos and three-dimensionally recreate them. This gives them a sense of space, place and action. They become a bridge between video and sculpture.

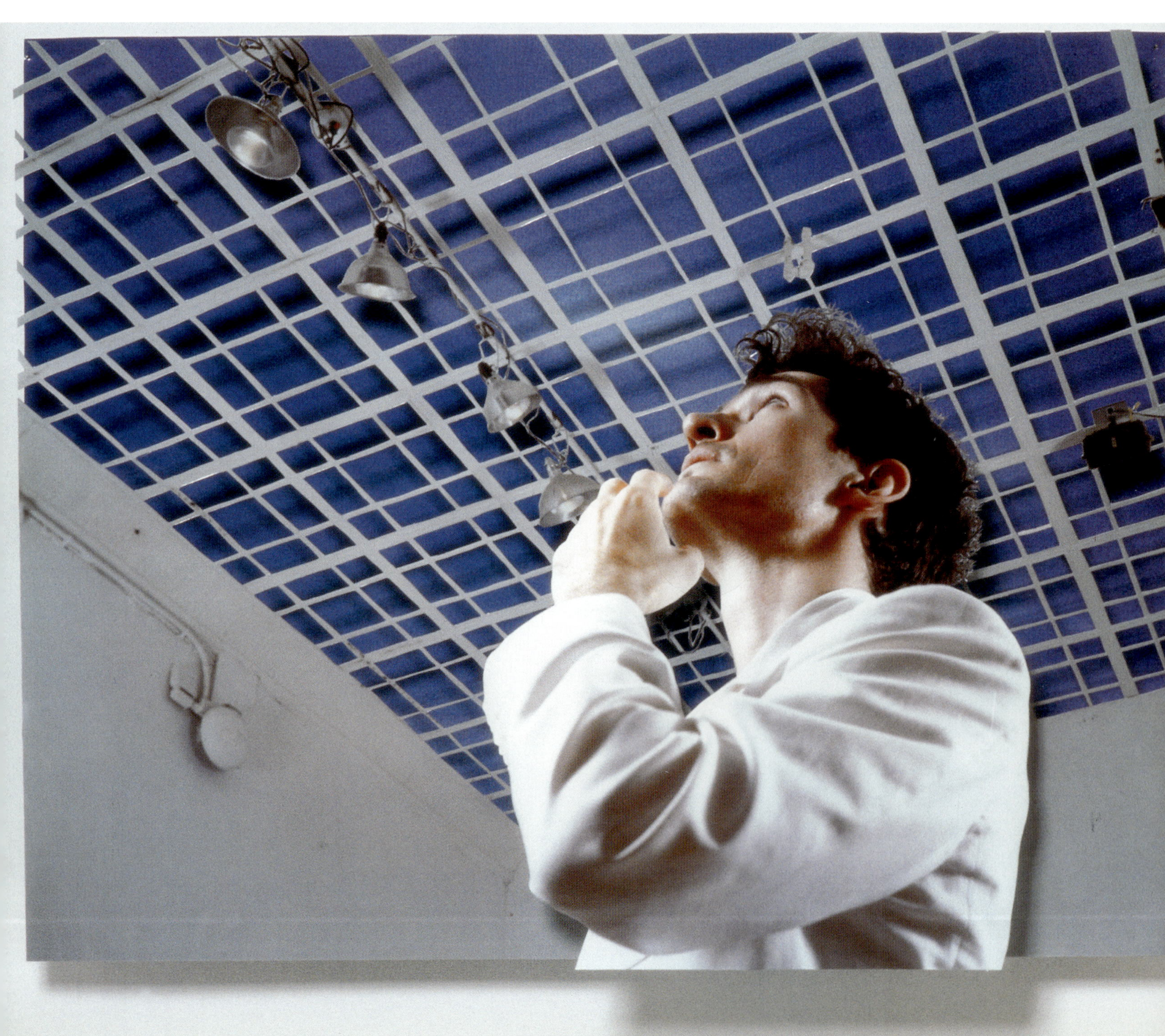

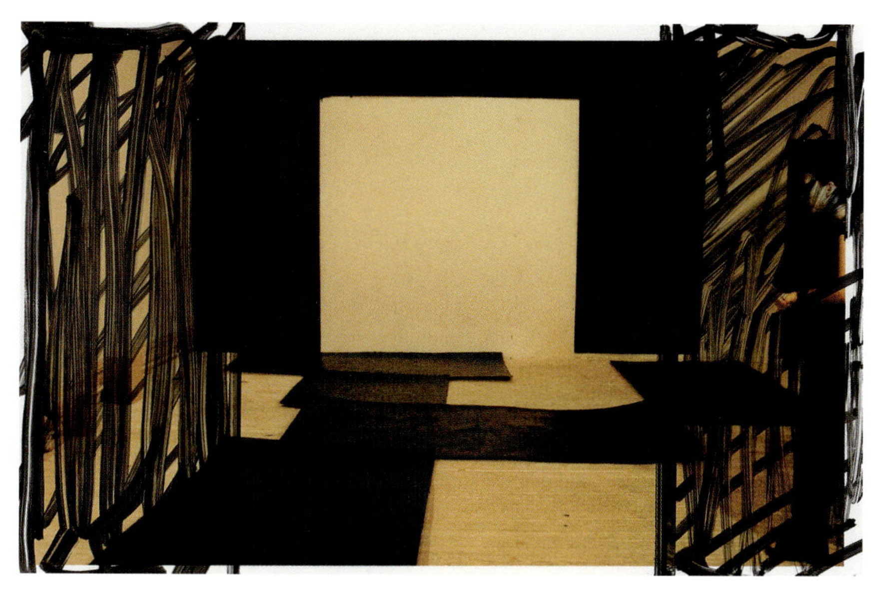

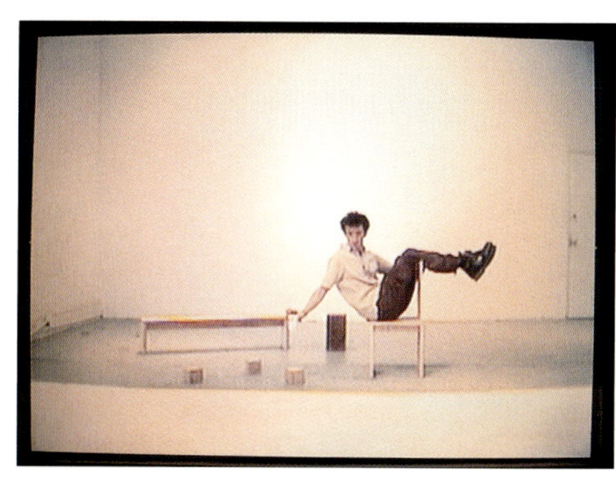

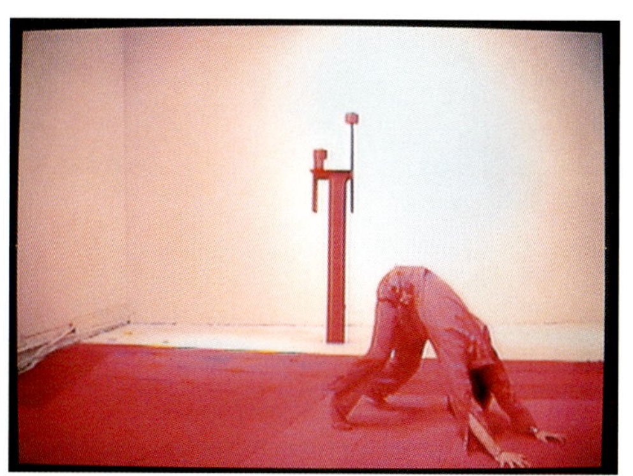

Sometimes it is the sets that help me to bridge from one medium to the next. The set above is from "Sleepless Nights". It is the first shot I took after lunch break and before filling the space again with actors. That set as seen through a camera lens seems exaggeratedly two dimensional -- an illusion I sometimes nurture. In this case I put a figure in it which transforms the surface into space.

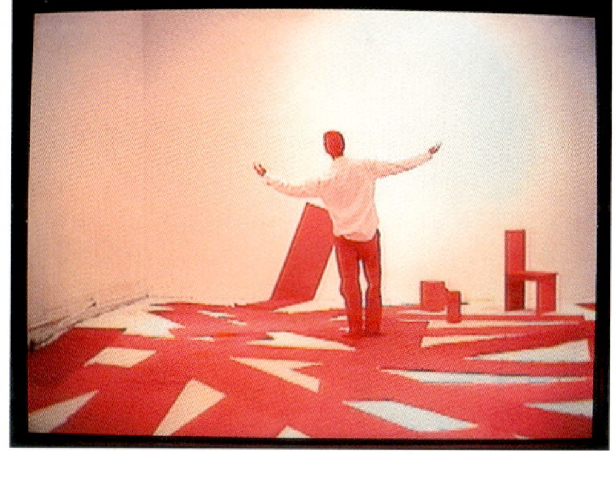

These live sketches demonstrate the build-up to one such moment. On the following page two figures are animated by the everchanging Mondrian-esque two dimensional architecture. Their poses respond to the shapes that surround them and the color of their clothing changes depending on what color they are standing on.

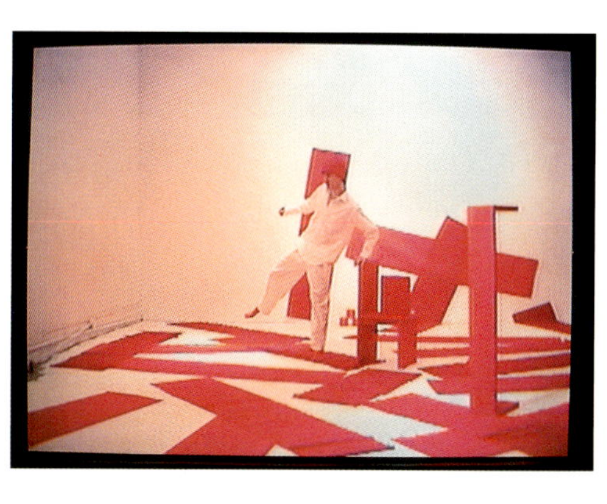

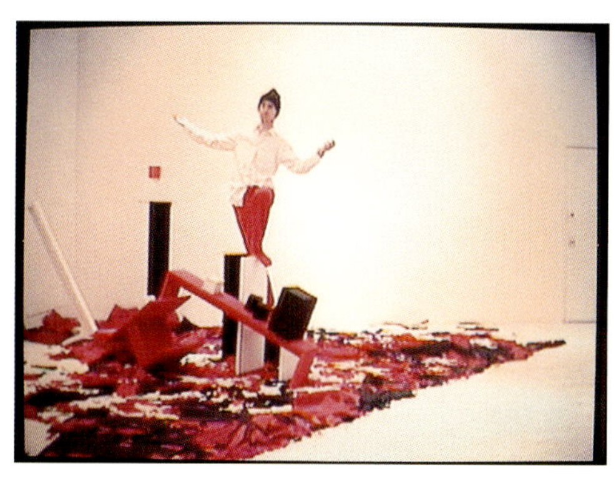

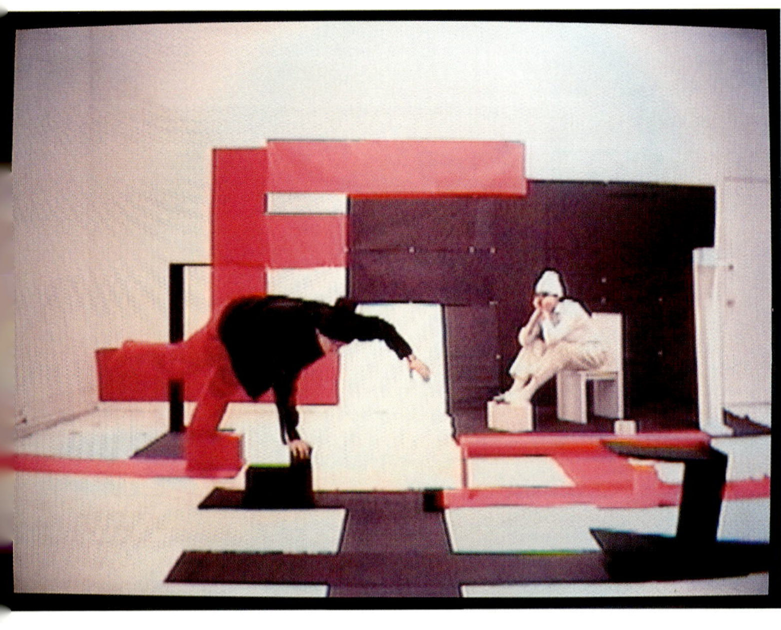

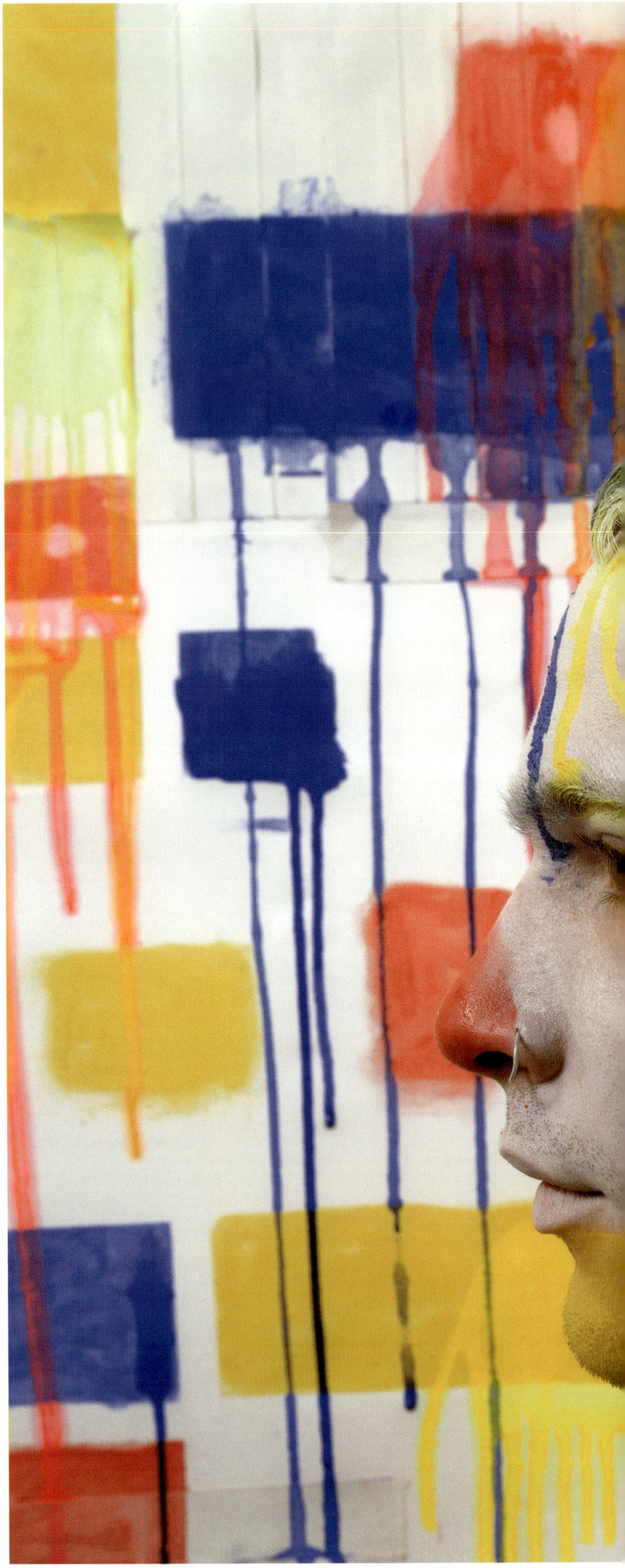

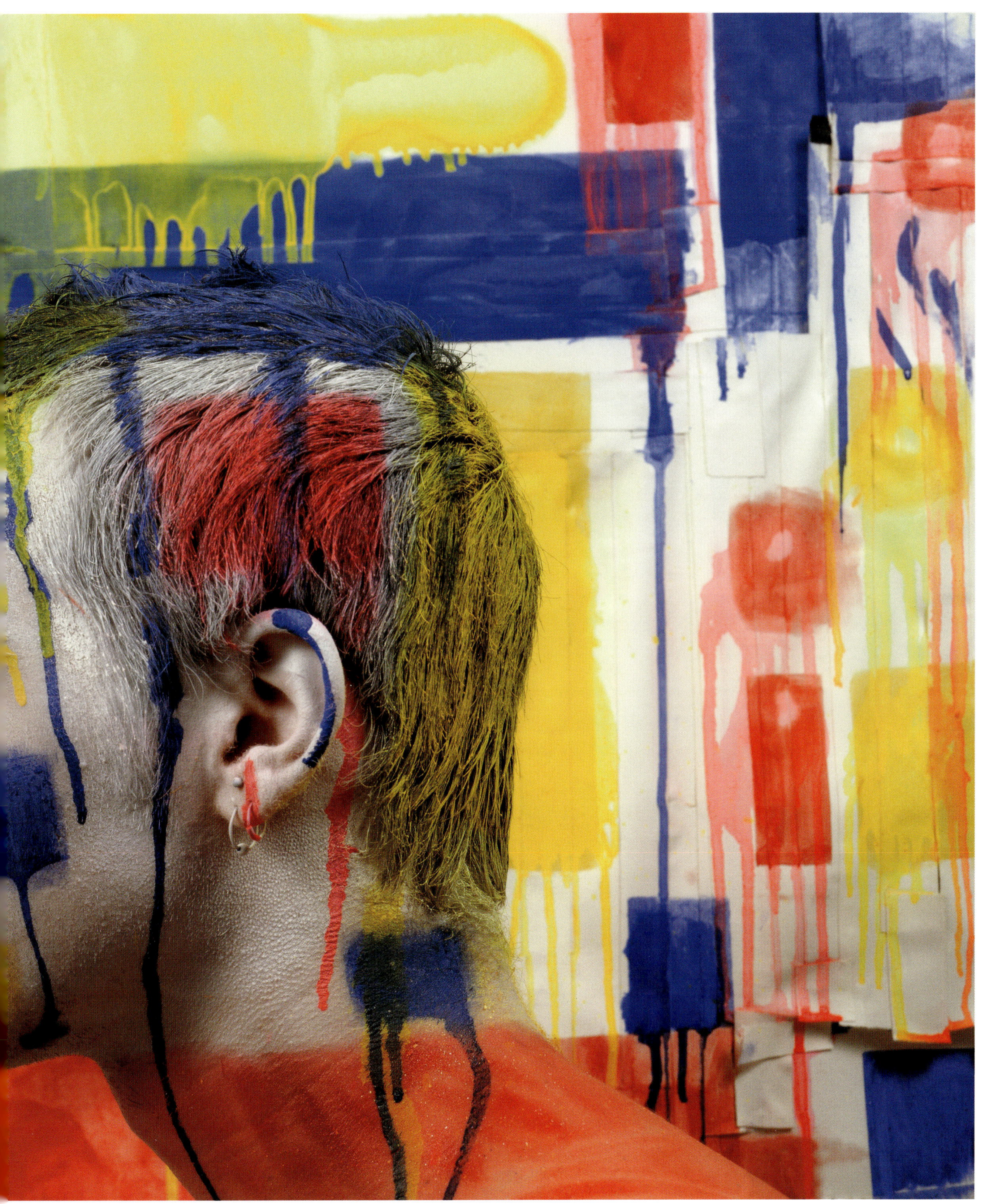

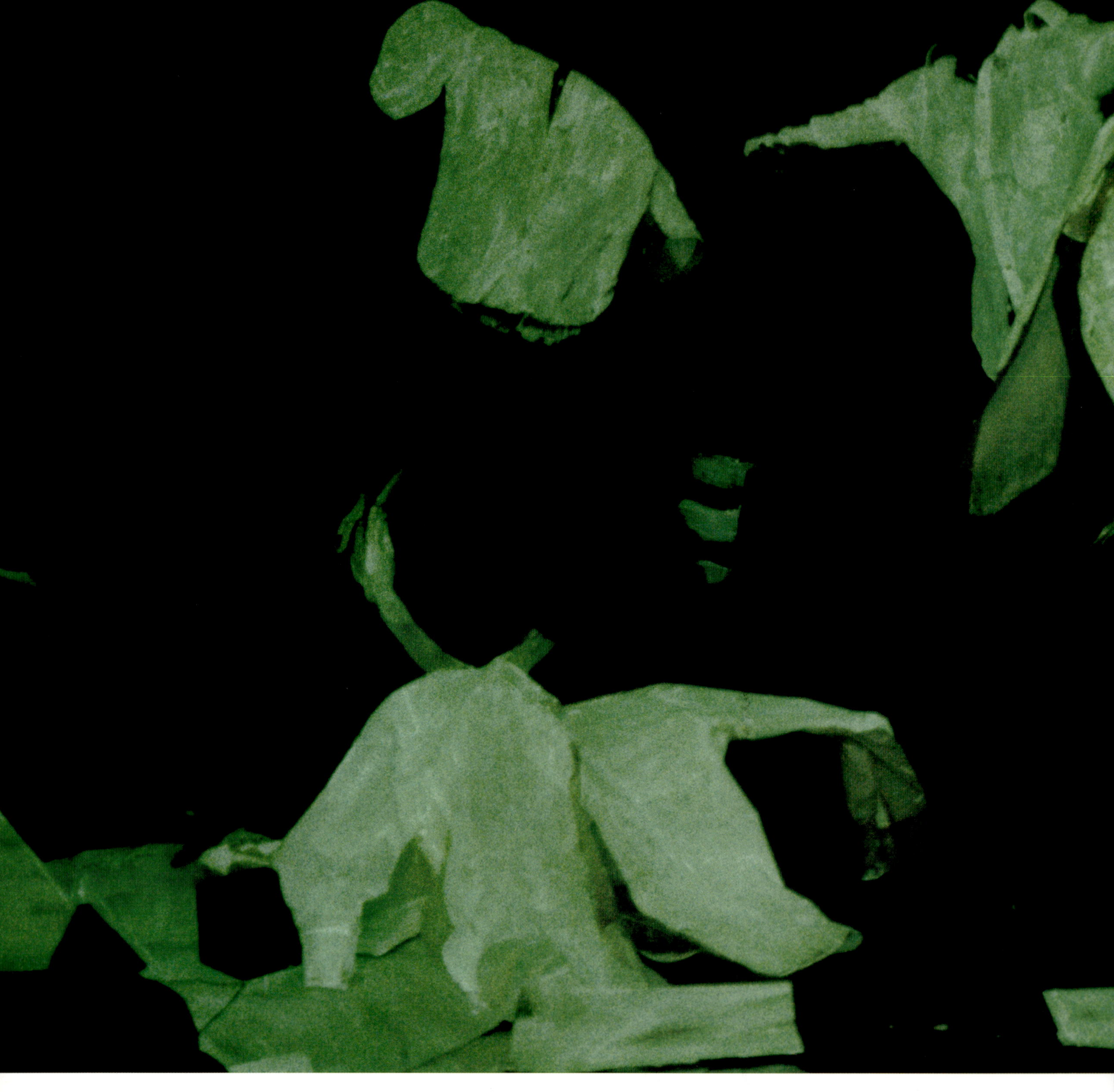

In "Little Dances of Misfortunes" and an unfinished video sketch, I work with abstraction and representation, playing them off each other by continuously concealing and revealing forms. In "Little Dances...", figures dissolve into the darkness, in the unfinished sketch, only parts of a body are exposed.

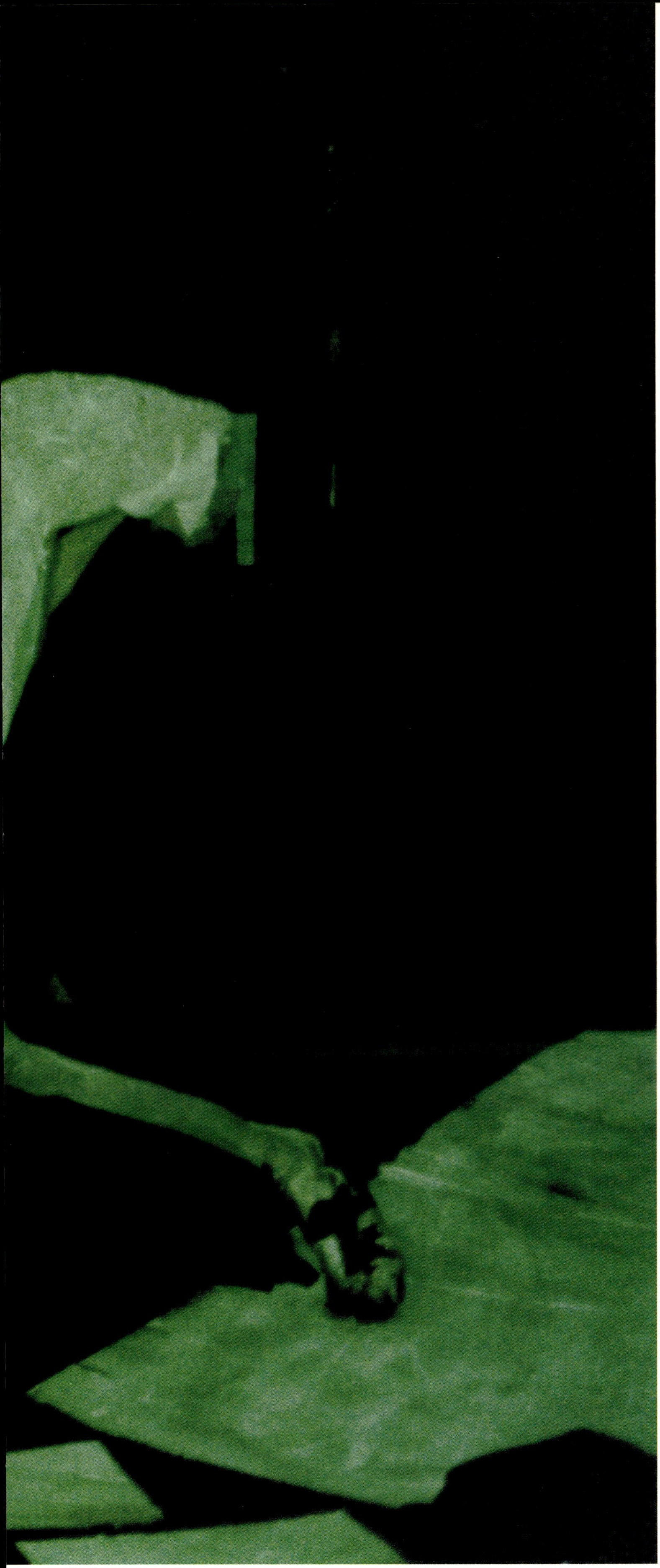

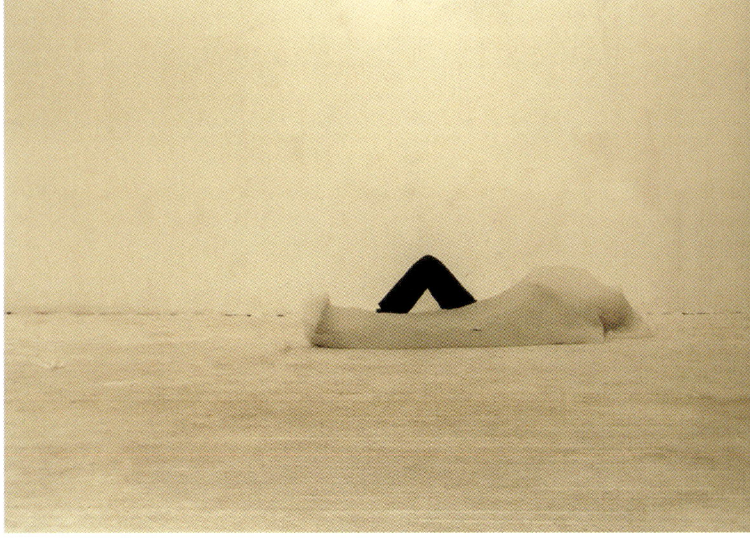
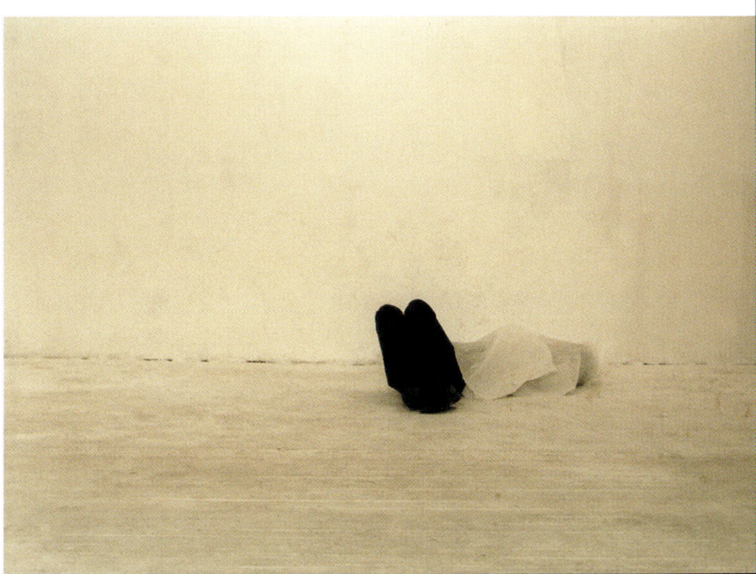

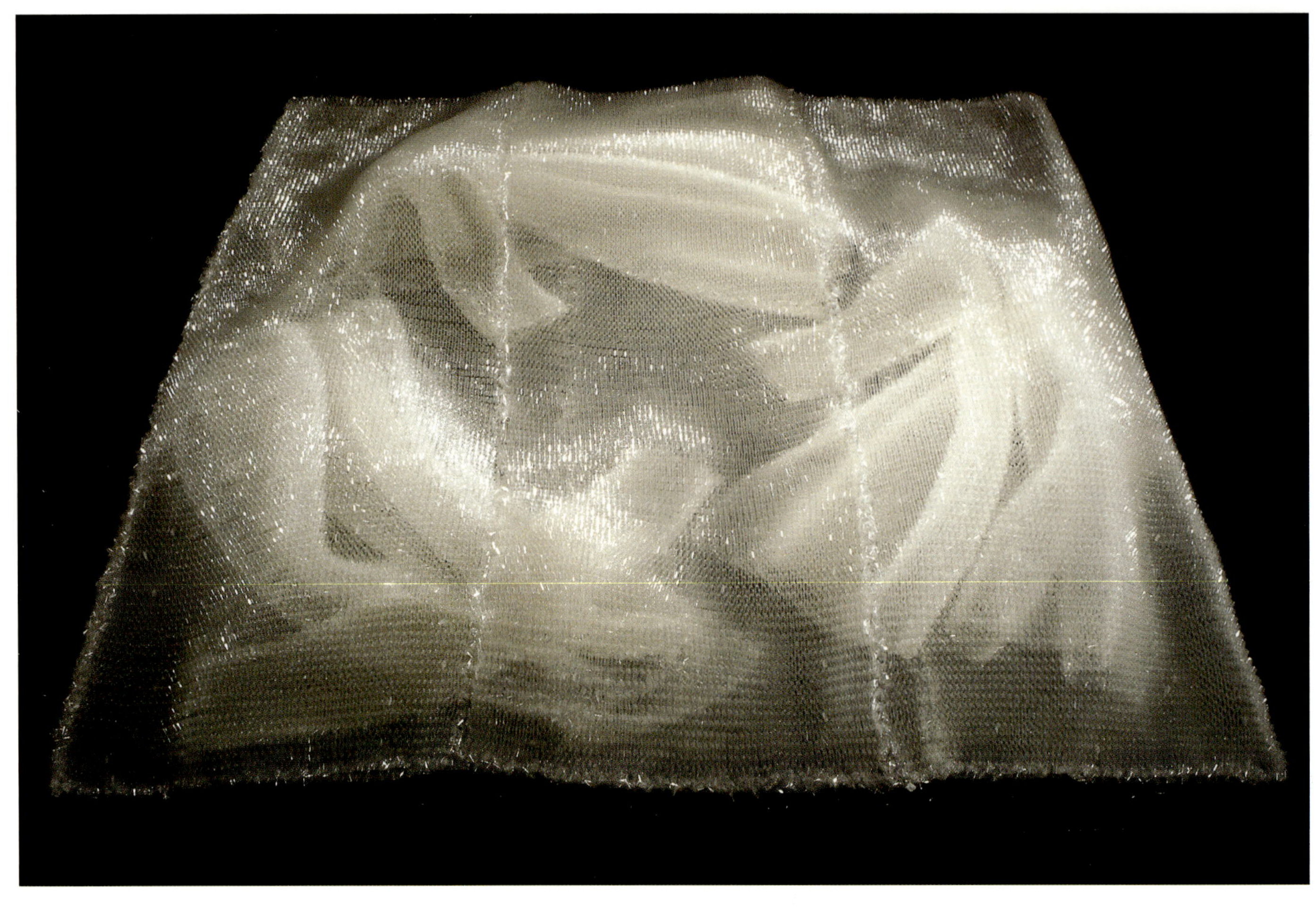

In "Raft", three coats seem to circle the mattress they are embedded in. The catch is that one can only really see them together from above. As the viewer walks around the piece the coats appear and disappear.

"Minefield and Wallflower" is another piece that animates a space below the obvious surface. To me it always looks like the exposed substructure of the wall it is set into. It is made with paper and multiple layers of white gouache that cakes over many of the gaps between the stitches. This further creates a sense of confusion between what is wall and what is not.

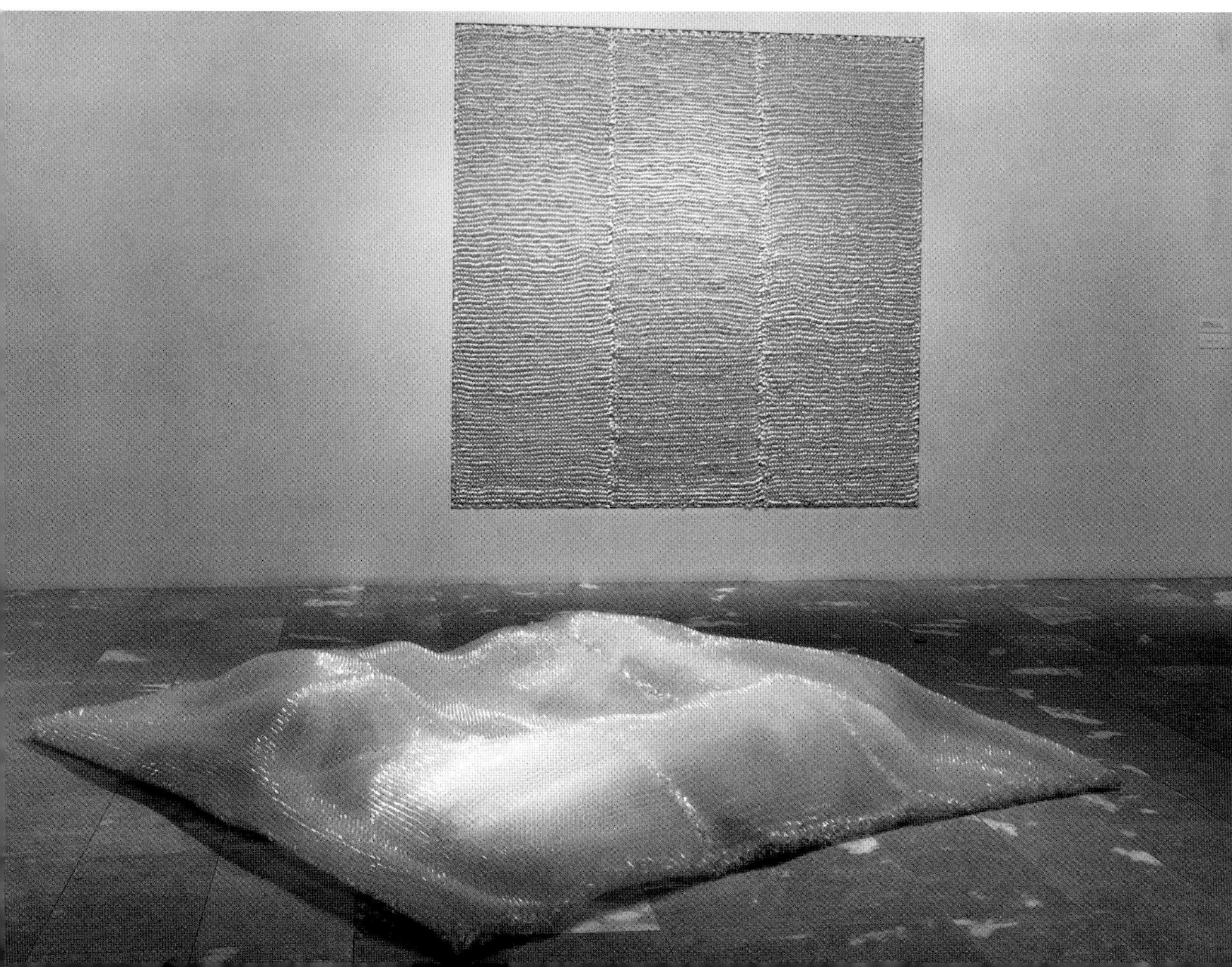

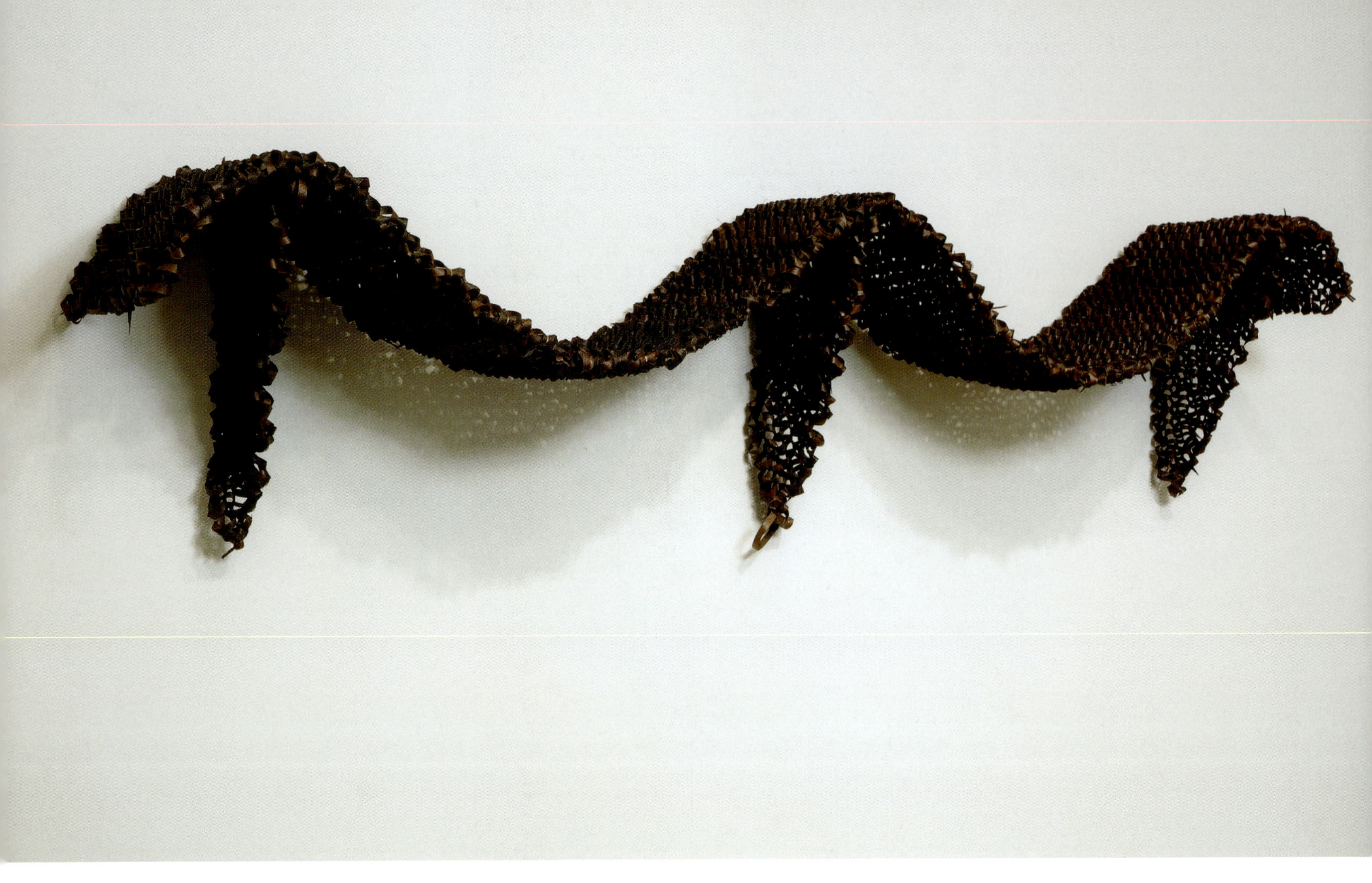

My wood sculptures all reference pieces of furniture,
chairs, shelfes, etc. – objects which in their most common
form are made from wood. By making these objects from
wood, but subjecting them to the unlikely process of
being knit, the functionality has been rendered function-
less.

Knit wood is quite soft since individual stitches
are separated by equal amounts of gaps. The soft
wooden fabric reacts to gravity by its own weight. The
hard and stable wood has been transformed into a soft
and unstable substance.

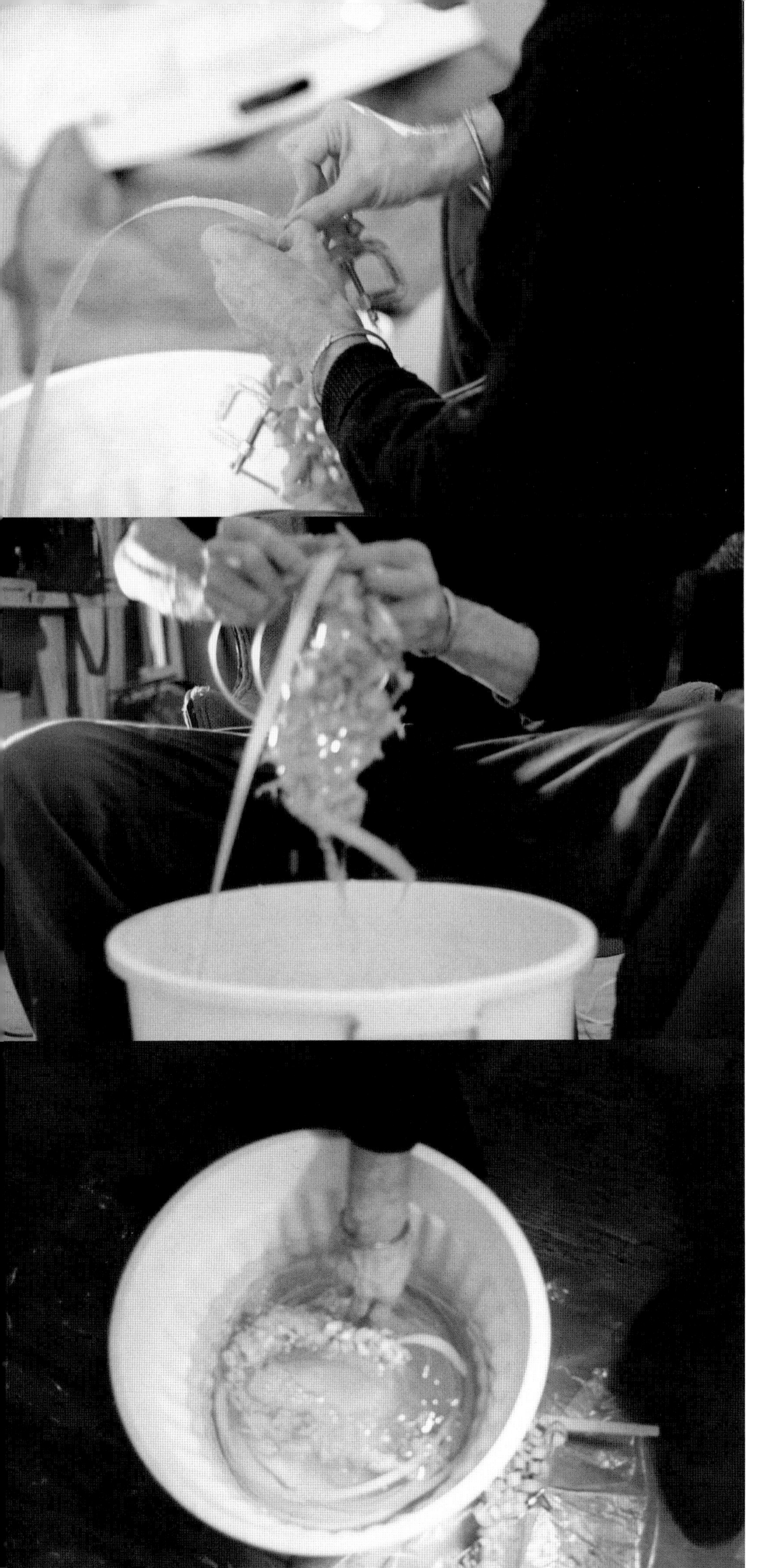

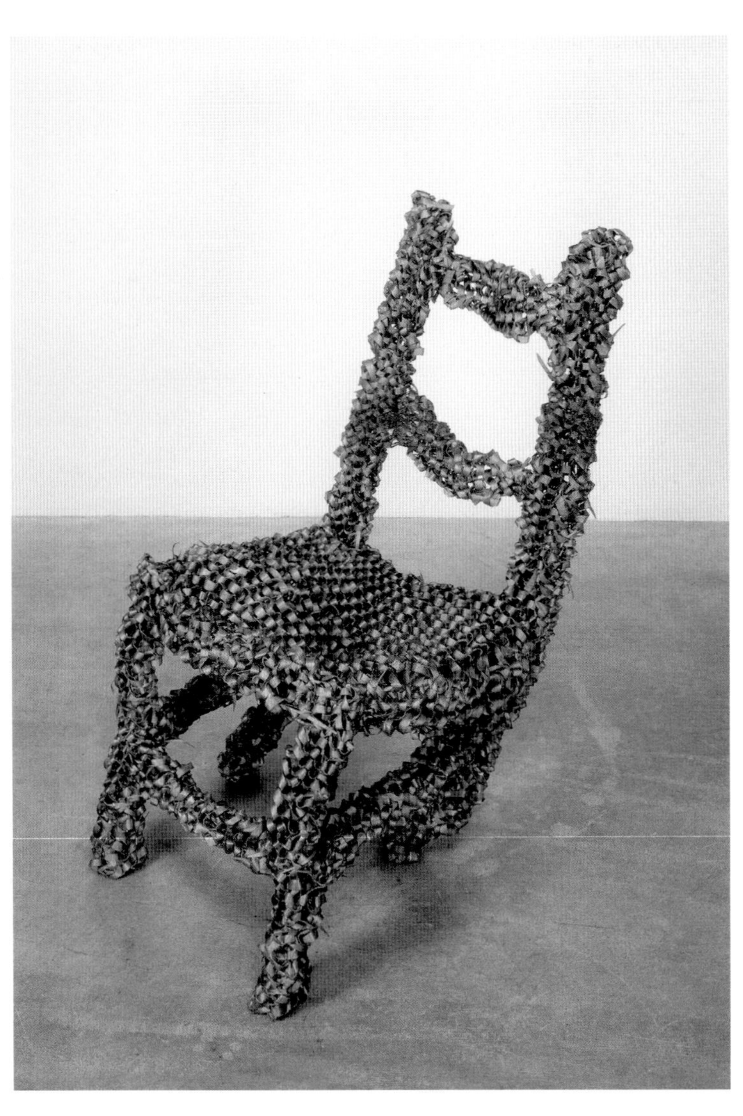

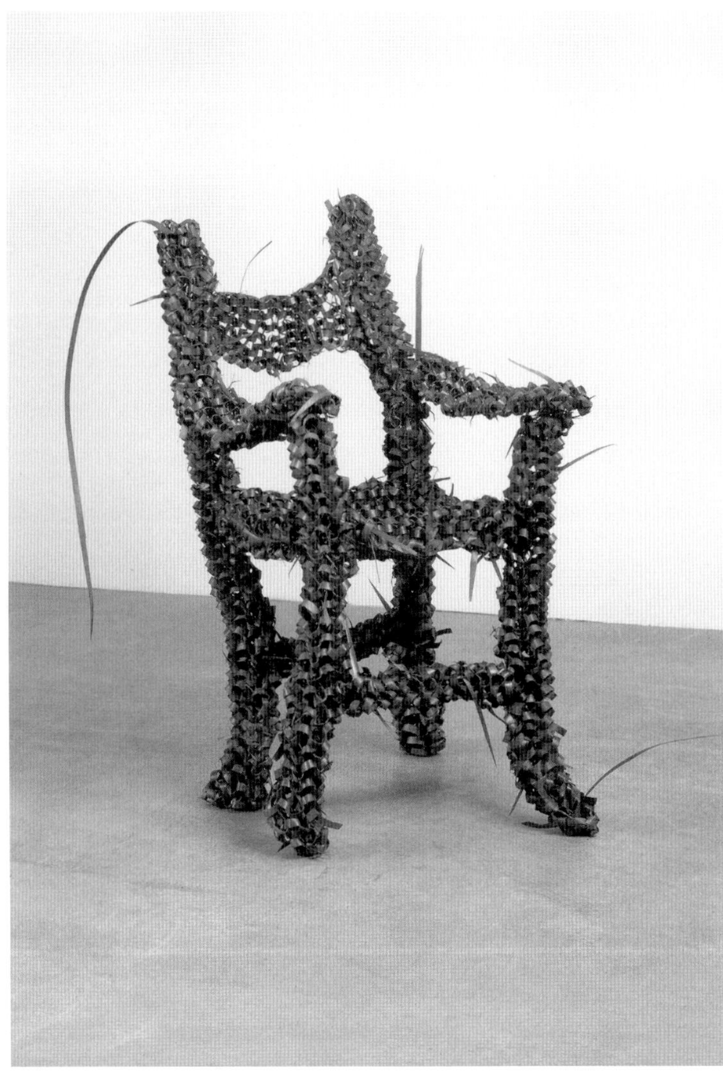

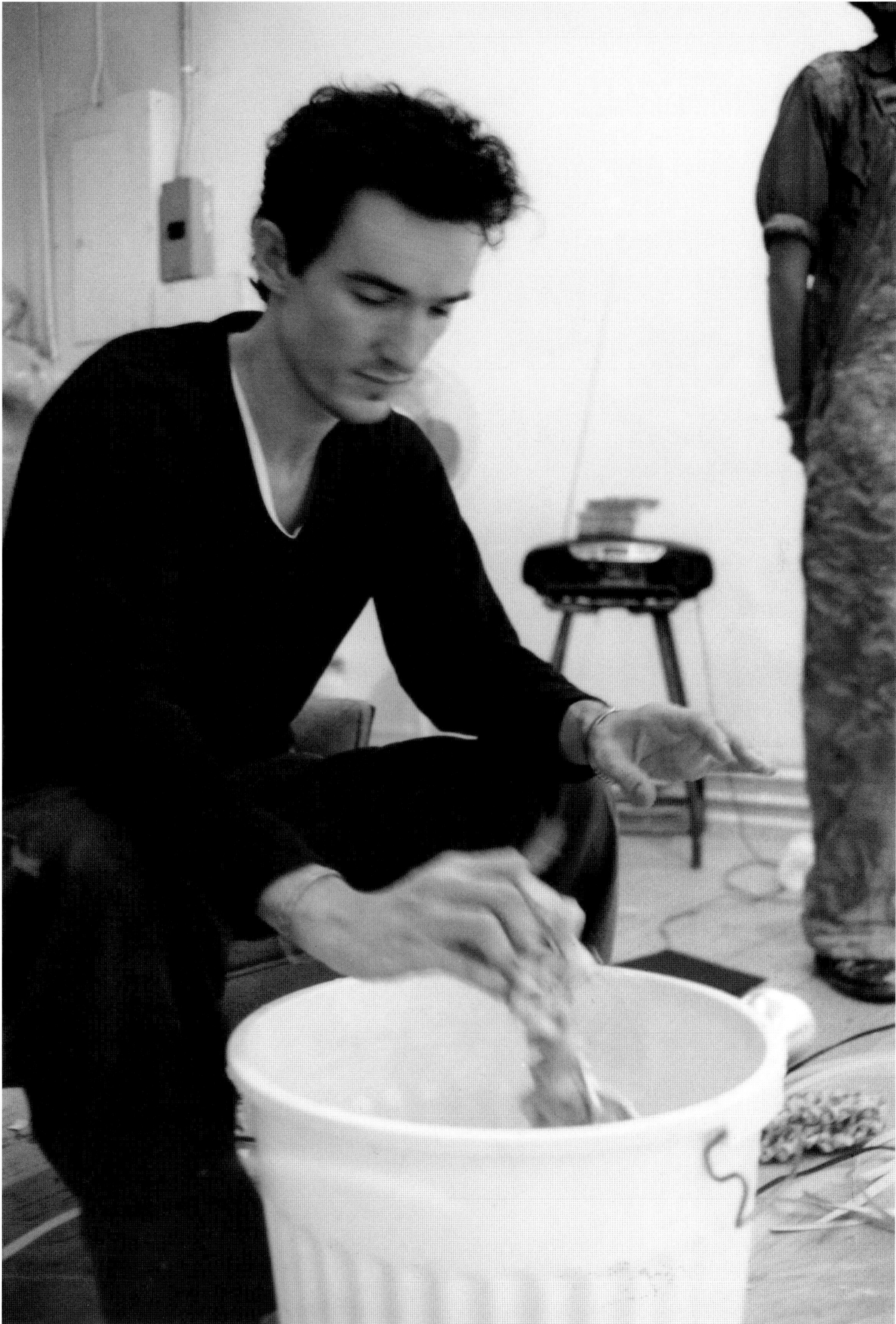

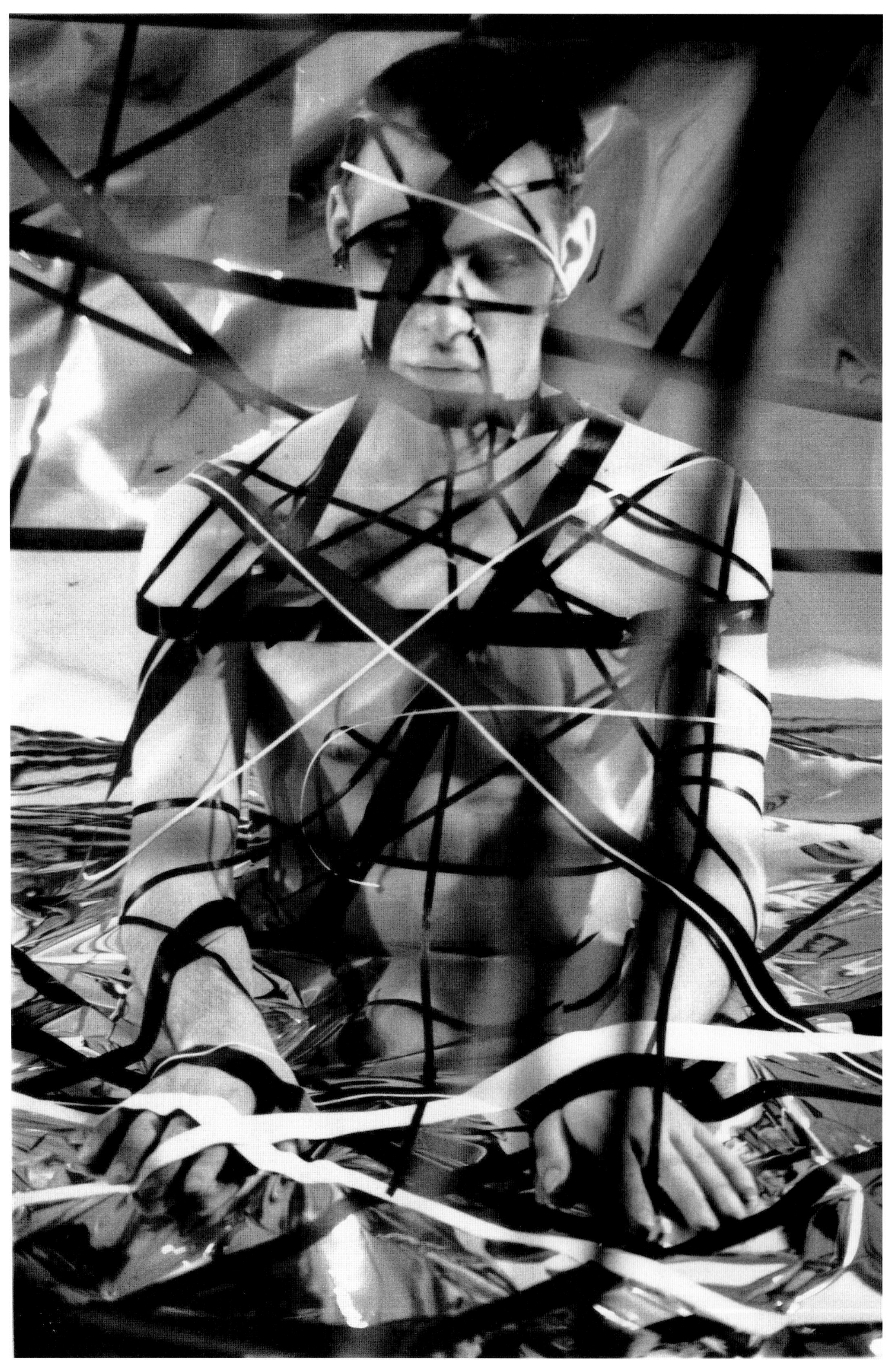

One of the more layered sequences from "The Sum and its Parts". I shot this in

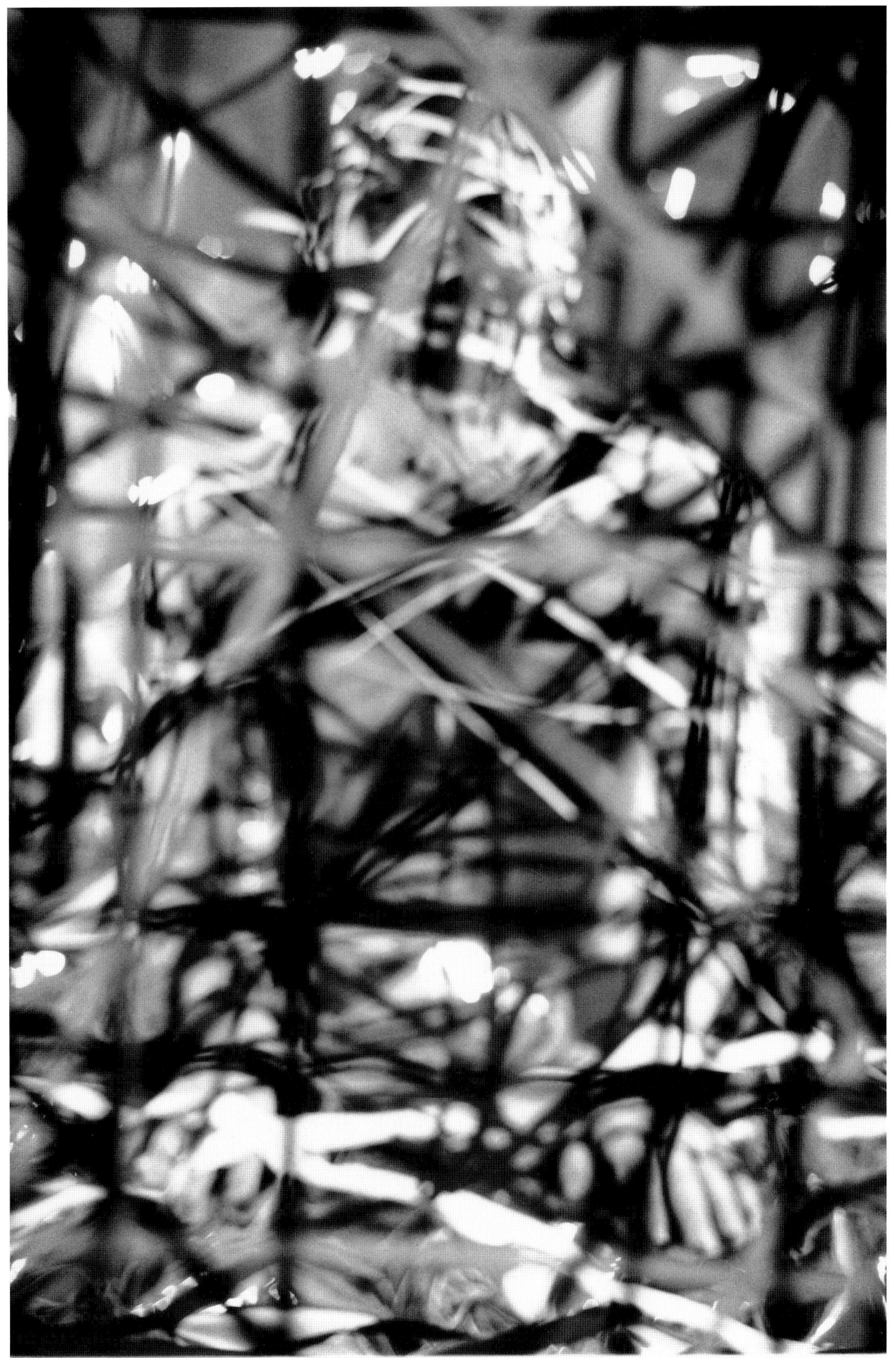

black and white to create more abstraction, but also in homage to Giacometti whose drawings inspired this scene.

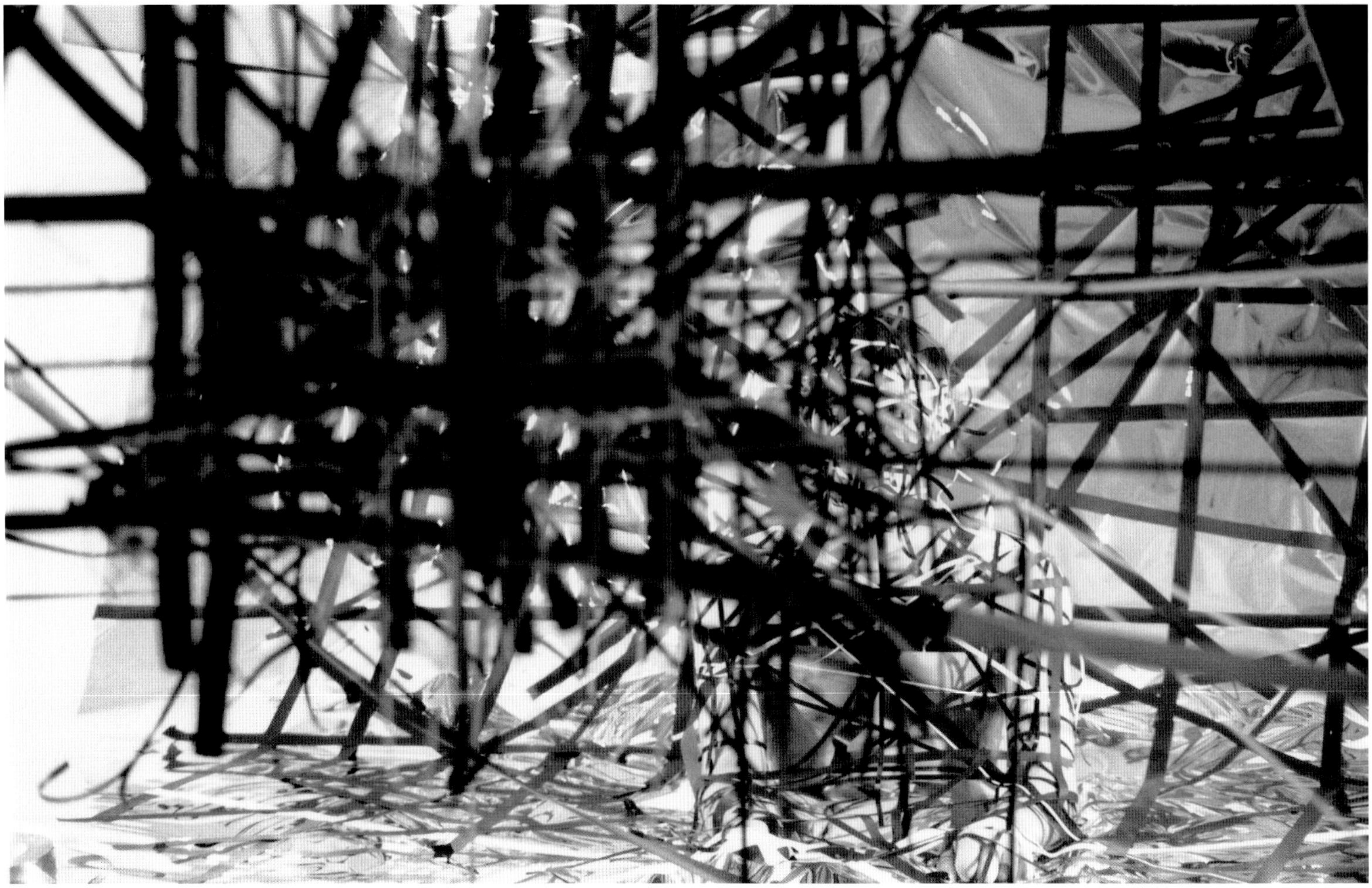

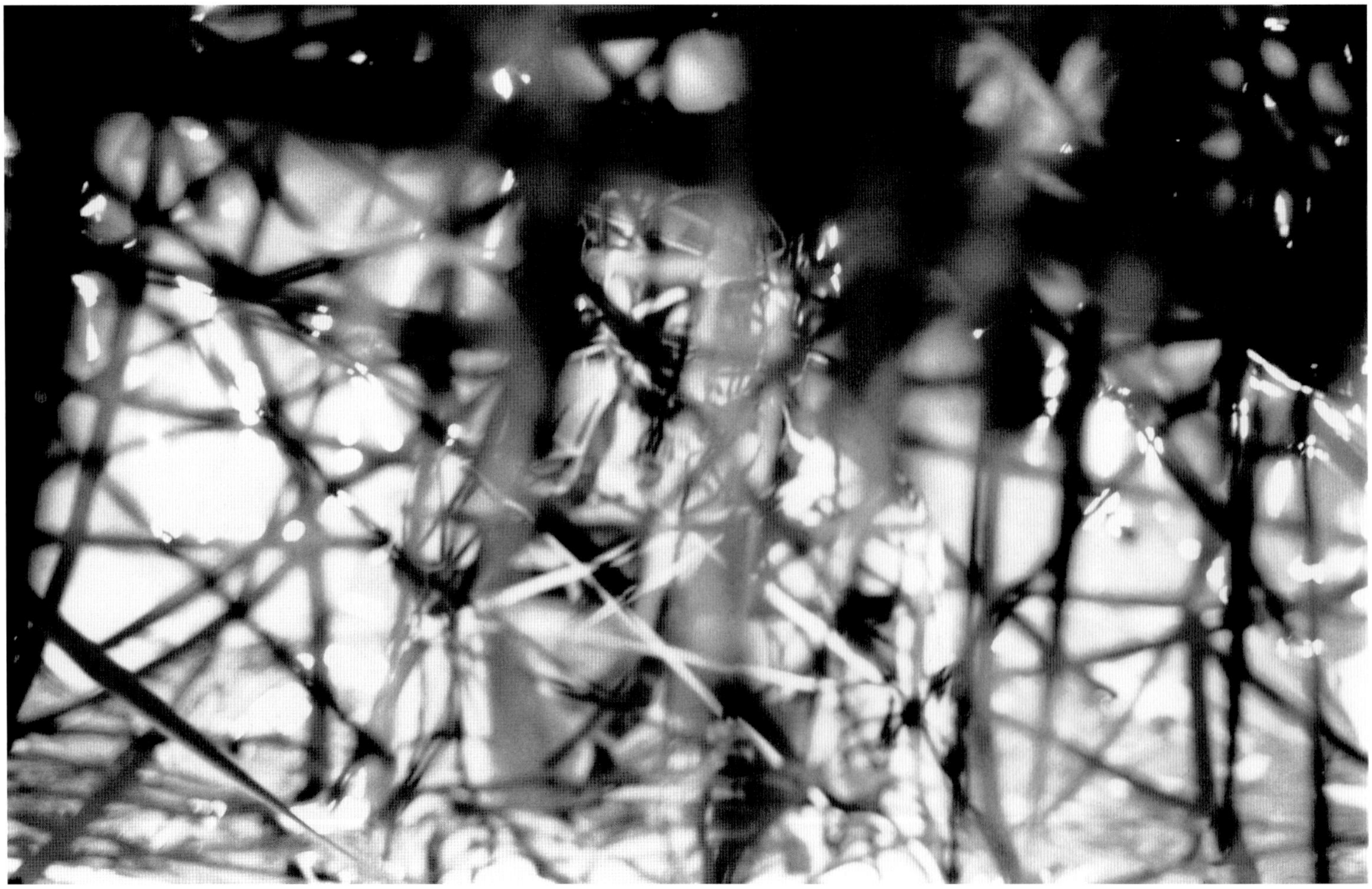

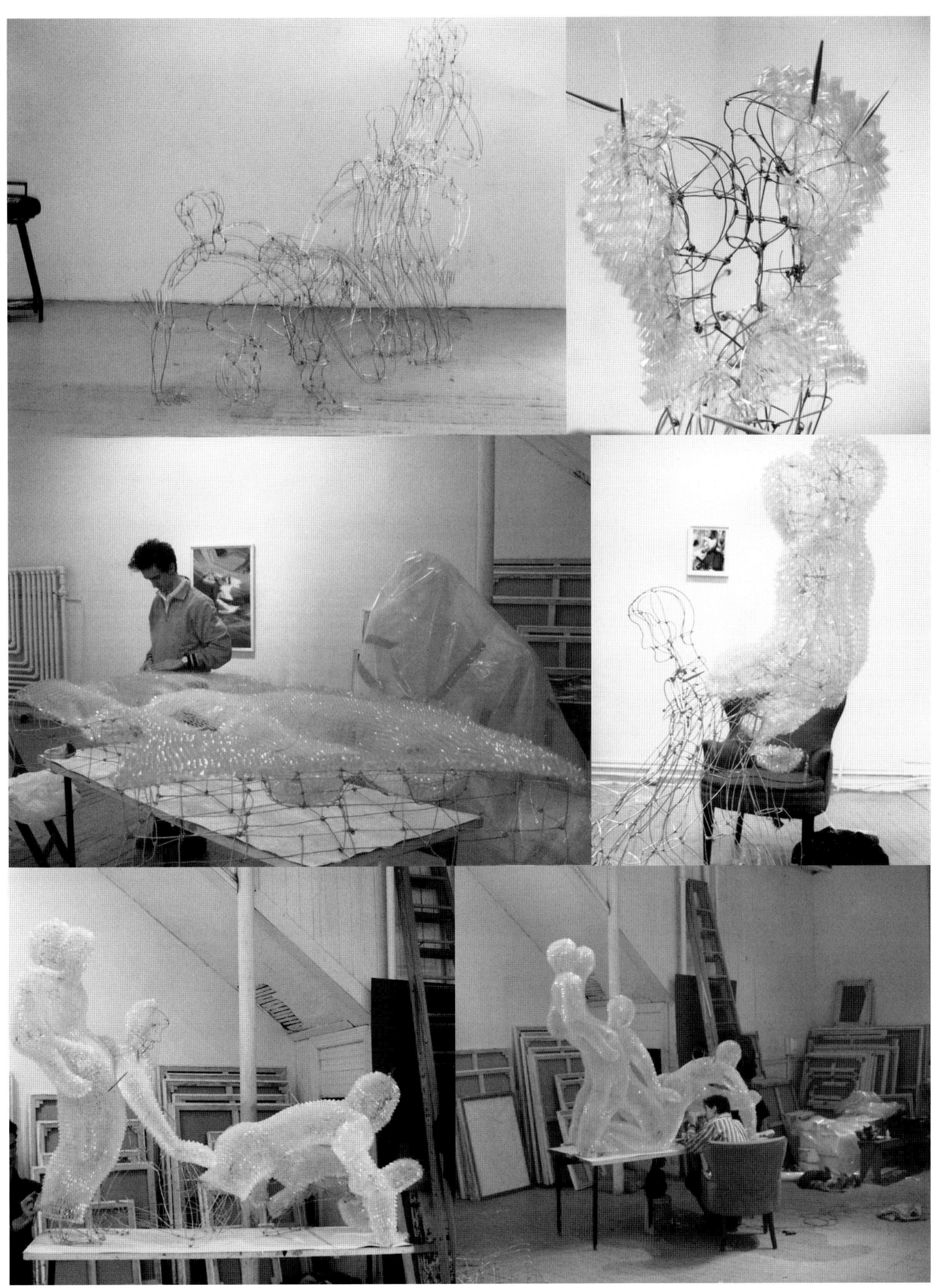

Working on "Soft Landing", (1999).

Derived from video stills "Soft Landing" depicts a figure in five stages of lulling,- one layered

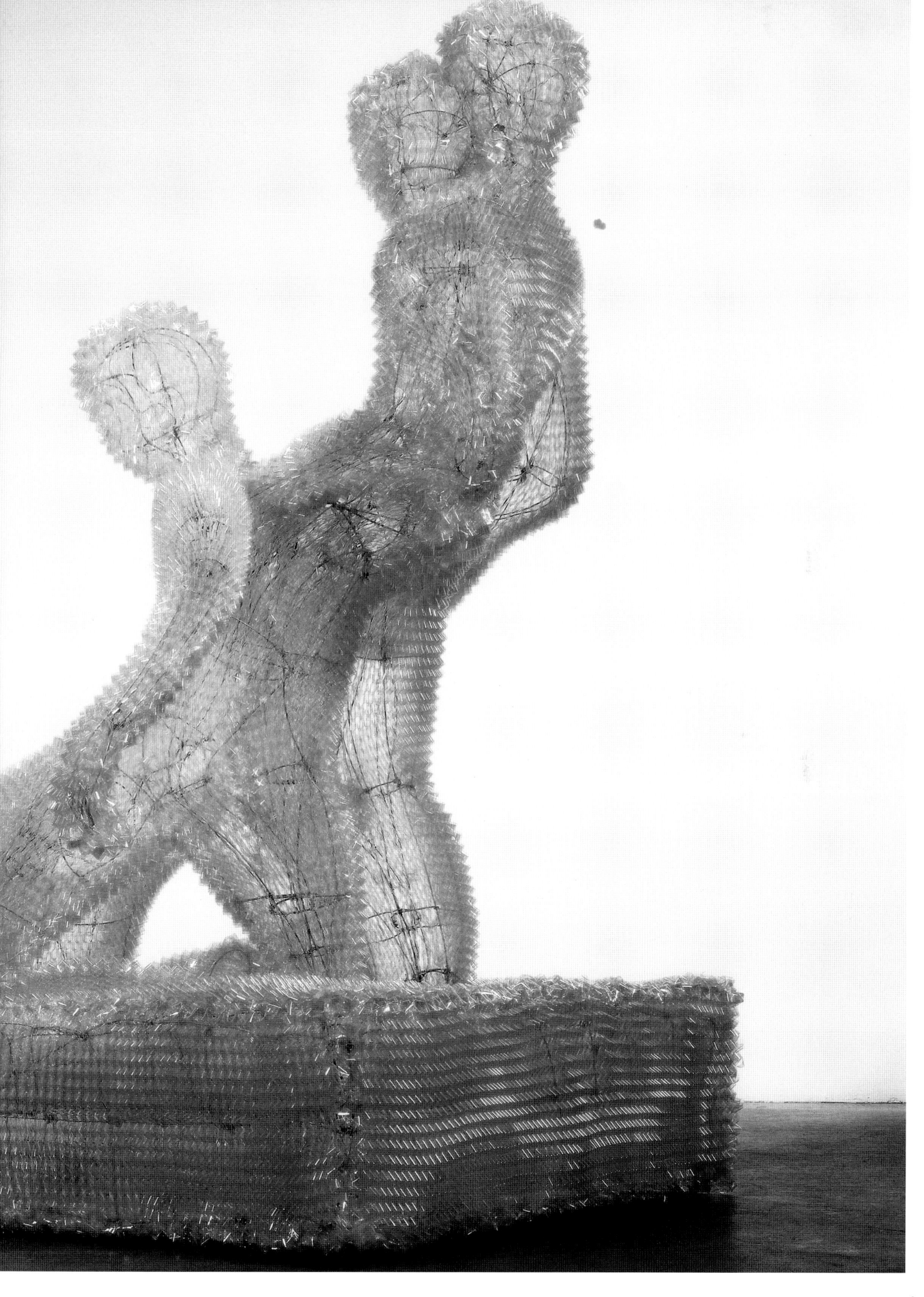

on top of the other. To make this piece I drew on all the mediums I work in,—sculpture, drawing, video, photography and performance.

IMAGES

page 1 Video still from **Videosketch #5**, 2001

2–3 The studio in which it all happens.

4–5 Color photograph from **Sleepless Nights**, 2001

6 Notes for the opening shot of **Sleepless Nights**, 2001

8 Sketch for **The Big Round Abstract Representational**, 2001

11 Snapshots of the artist working on **The Big Round Abstract Representational**, 2001. Silver Mylar, nylon, and Styrofoam, diameter six feet. Courtesy Oliver Herring and Max Protetch Gallery, New York

12 Seven photo cut-outs from **Exit**, 1999–2000

16 Six video stills from **Videosketch #5**, 2001

17 Color photograph from **Sleepless Nights**, 2001

18–19 Four color photographs from **Sleepless Nights**, 2001

20 Color photograph from **Sleepless Nights**, 2001

21 **Distorted Round #2**, 2001. Gold Mylar, 5 inches x 32 inches diameter. Courtesy Oliver Herring and Max Protetch Gallery, New York

22 **Queensize Bed with Coat**, 1993–94. Silver Mylar, nylon, and Styrofoam, 12 x 57 x 88 inches. Collection Eileen and Peter Norton

23 **Distorted Round #1**, 2001. Silver Mylar, 9 inches x 80 inches diameter. Courtesy Oliver Herring and Max Protetch Gallery, New York

24 top: **An Age for Hands**, 1996. Silver Mylar on steel, 9 feet x 13 feet x five inches. Courtesy Oliver Herring, Rhodes and Mann, London, and Max Protetch Gallery, New York
bottom: Color photograph from **Sleepless Nights**, 2001

25 **Distorted Round #2**, 2001. Gold Mylar, 5 inches x 32 inches diameter. Courtesy Oliver Herring and Max Protetch Gallery, New York.

26–27 Color photograph from **Sleepless Nights**, 2001

28 Eight color photographs from **Sleepless Nights**, 2001

29 Two color photographs from **Little Dances of Misfortunes**, 2001

30 Color photograph from **Sleepless Nights**, 2001

31 Color photograph from **Pure Sublimation**, 2000–2001

32 **A Flower for Ethyl Eichelberger**, 1991. Transparent tape, dimensions variable. Courtesy Oliver Herring

33 Color photograph from **Exit**, 1999–2000

34–35 Documentation for making **Exit**, 1999–2000

36–37 Four color photographs from **Exit**, 1999–2000

38 top: Color photograph from **The Sum and Its Parts**, 2001
bottom: Color photograph from **Little Dances of Misfortunes**, 2001

39 Three color photographs from **Two One-Day Sketches**, 2000

40 Color photograph from **Pure Sublimation**, 2000–2001

41 Color photograph from **Two One-Day Sketches**, 2000

42 top: Snapshot from the set of **Two One-Day Sketches**, 2000
bottom: Color photograph from **Two One-Day Sketches**, 2000

43 Color photograph from **Sketch for Little Dances of Misfortunes**, 2001

44–45 Three color photographs from **Little Dances of Misfortunes**, 2001

46 Sketch #2 for **Double Rocker**, 1999. Marker on Mylar, 18 x 24 inches. Collection Kent and Vicki Logan

47 top: **Distorted Round #1**, 2001. Silver Mylar, 9 x 80 inches diameter. Courtesy Oliver Herring and Max Protetch Gallery, New York
bottom: Two views of **Double Rocker**, 1999. Silver Mylar and wire, 44 x 24 x 50 inches. Collection Kent and Vicki Logan

48–49 Two color photographs from **The Sum and Its Parts**, 2001

50 top: Color photograph from **The Sum and Its Parts**, 2001
bottom left: **Multiple Fake**, 1997. Transparent Mylar, 64 x 64 x 24 inches. Private Collection
bottom right: Color photograph from **Two One-Day Sketches**, 2000

51 top: **Castle**, 1994. Transparent Mylar, 64 x 47 x 9 inches. Collection Kent and Vicki Logan

bottom left: Color photograph of performance **Framed by Darkess**, 1995

bottom right: **Fossil**, 1995. Transparent Mylar, 64 x 64 x 24 inches. Private collection

52 **Covered Coat #1**, 1994. Silver Mylar, 84 x 78 inches. Collection Kristi and Dean Jernigan

53 **Covered Coat #2**, 1994. Transparent Mylar, 78 x 72 inches. Private collection

54–55 Three color photographs from **Pure Sublimation**, 2000–2001

56 **Exit 3-D Still #2**, 2000. Cibachrome, 16 x 20 x 3 inches. Collection Greg Miller

57 Color photograph from **Sleepless Nights**, 2001; Five video stills from Videosketch #4, 1999

58 Video still from **Videosketch #4**, 1999

59 Color photograph from **The Sum and Its Parts**, 2001

60 Color photograph from **Little Dances of Misfortunes**, 2001

61 Two color photographs from an unfinished video

62 **Raft**, 1995. Transparent Mylar, 84 x 88 inches. Collection Mr. Hideyuki Osawa

63 **Minefield and Wallflower**, 1995. Paper and paper pulp, 88 x 88 inches. Collection Mr. Hideyuki Osawa

64 **Shelf**, 1999. White Birch and Mahogany stain, 21 x 89 x 13inches. Collection Mr. Hideyuki Osawa

65 Three snapshots of the artist working on one of the chairs

66 top: **Untitled (Chair #1)**, 1999. White Birch, Oak stain, wire, 41 x 18 x 18 inches. Collection Eileen and Peter Norton

bottom: **Untitled (Chair #3)**, 2000. White birch, American Walnut stain, wire, 38 x 22 x 25 inches. Collection Kristi and Dean Jernigan

67 Snapshot of the artist working with wood

68–69 Two black and white photographs from **The Sum and Its Parts**, 2001

70 Two black and white photographs from **The Sum and Its Parts**, 2001

71 Snapshots of the artist working on **Soft Landing**, 1999

72–73 **Soft Landing**, 1999. Transparent Mylar and wire, 78 x 117 x 48 inches. Collection Eileen and Peter Norton.

76–77 Performers top row (left to right): Miek Coccia, Joyce Pensato, Brandon Greenbaum, David Kalka, Starr Figura, and Filip Noterdaeme; second row (left to right): Sascha Davis, Davis Thompson-Moss, Fran Ferraro, Davide Borella, Javier Piñòn, and Brian Reedy; third row (left to right): Cecilia Dean, Nancy Yousef, Caroline Duval-Arnould, Tracy, Christopher Dorland, Elizabeth Kley, and Cheryl Horsfall; bottom row (left to right): Mary-Helen Harvey, Jeffrey Sperber, Jenny Frost, Luis Moreno, Mitchell Marco, Matthew Goodwrich and Peter Krashes

80 **Lifeline Rolled Up**, 1992–1994. Knit silver Mylar, 21 x 29 x 470 inches unrolled. Private Collection

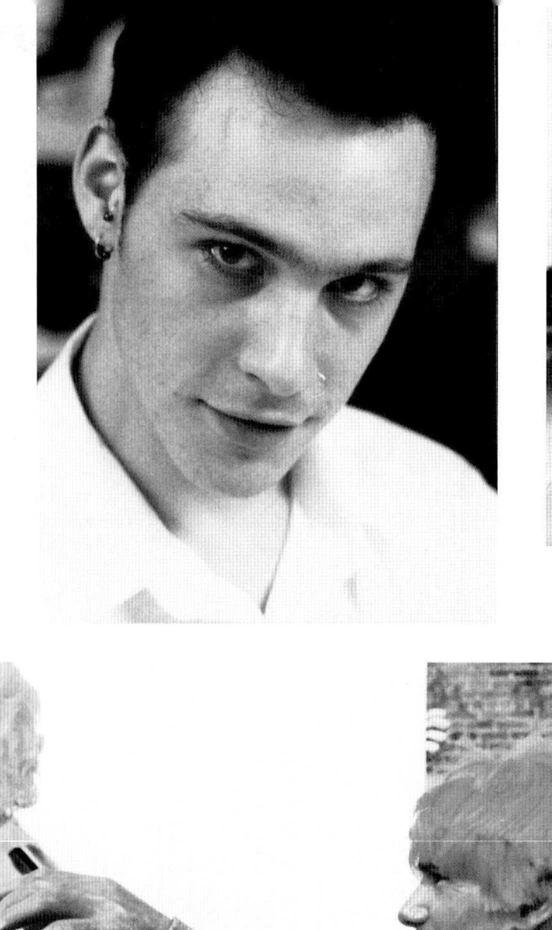
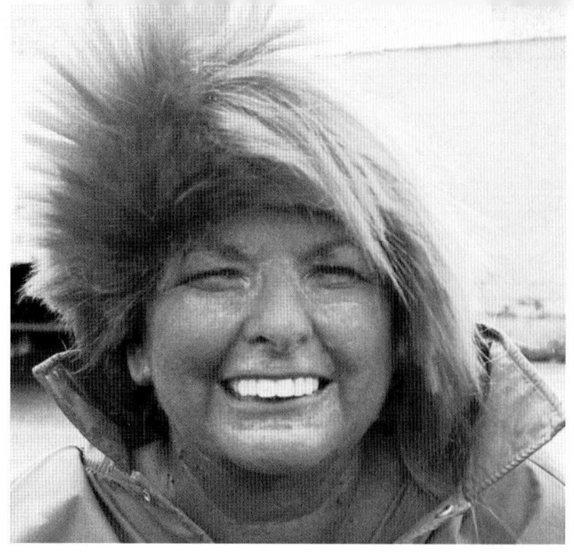
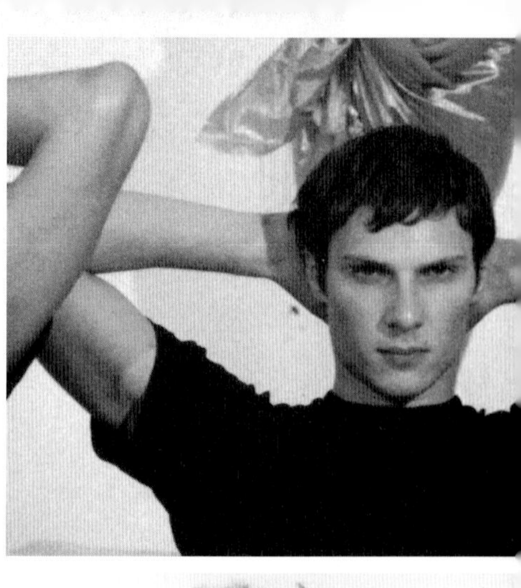
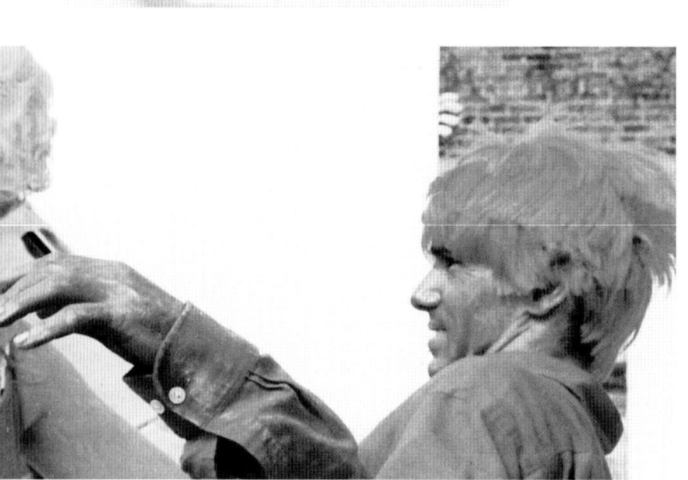
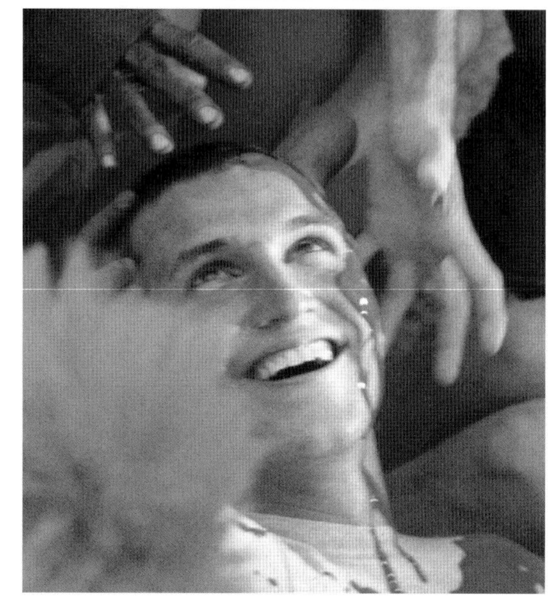
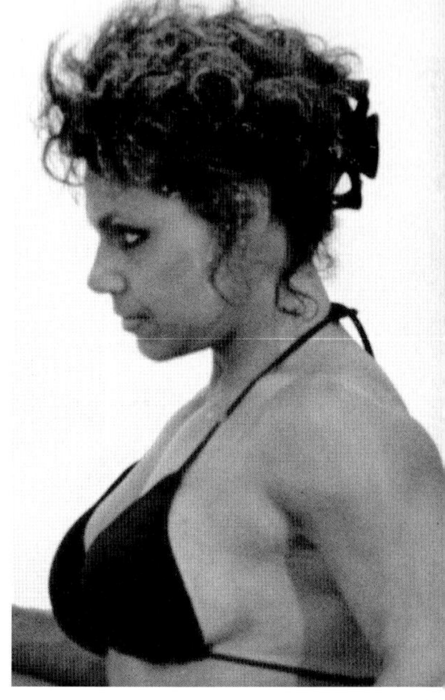
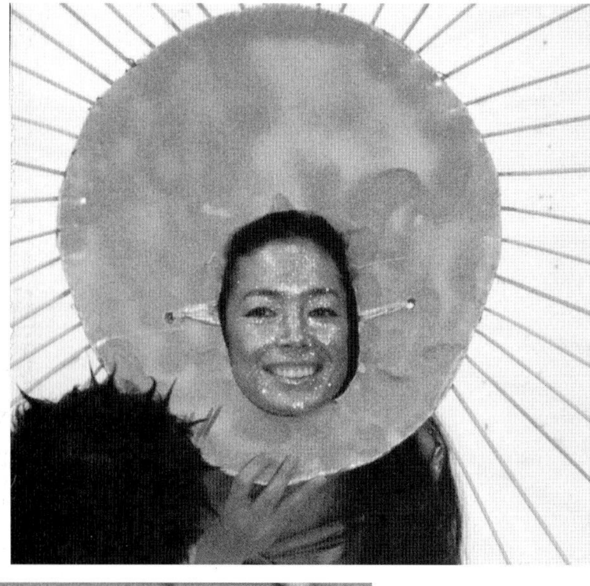
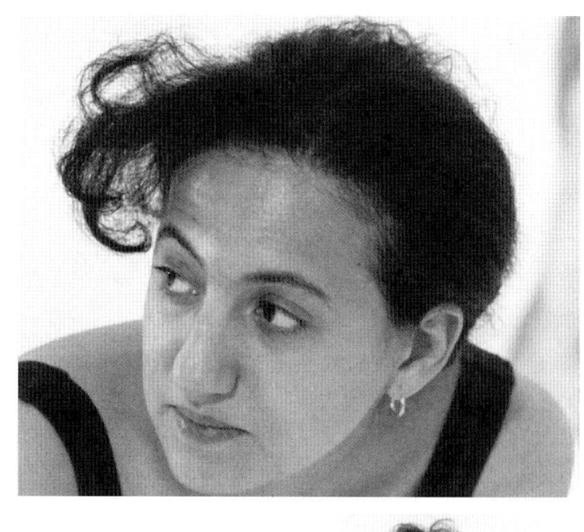
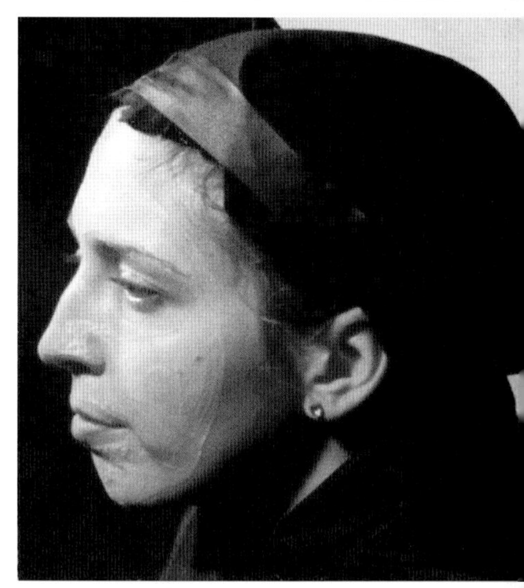
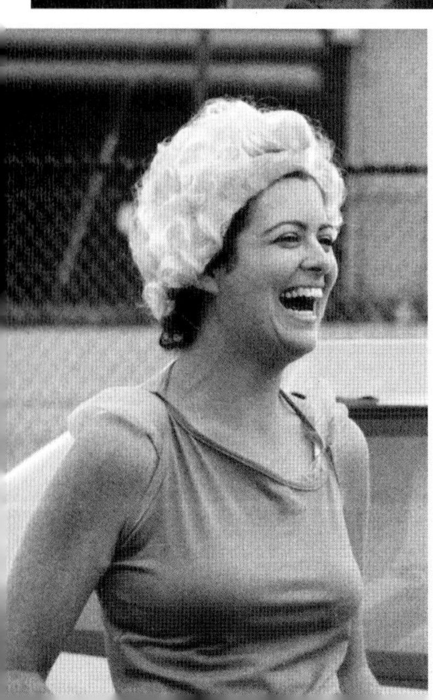
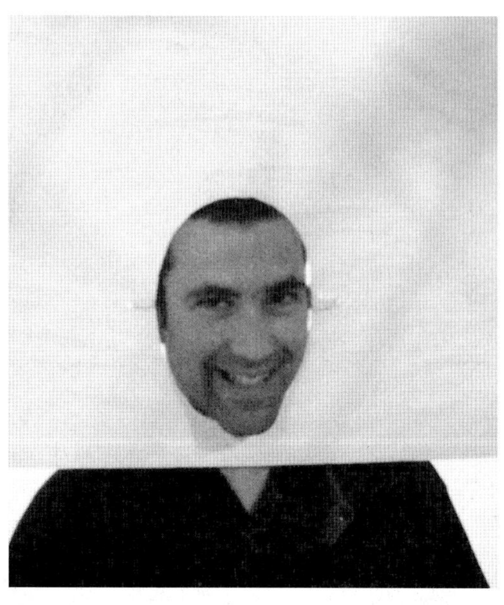
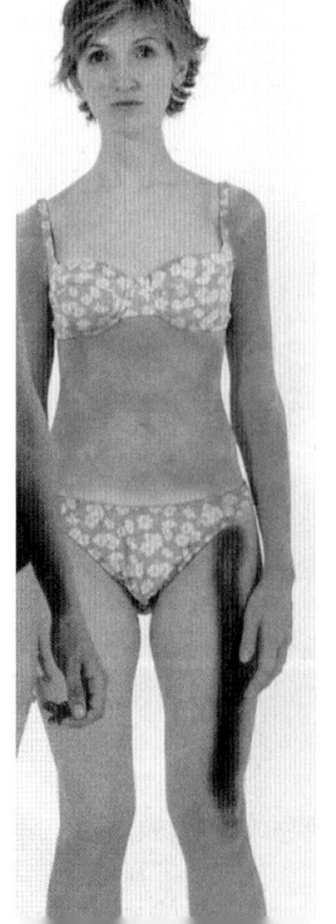
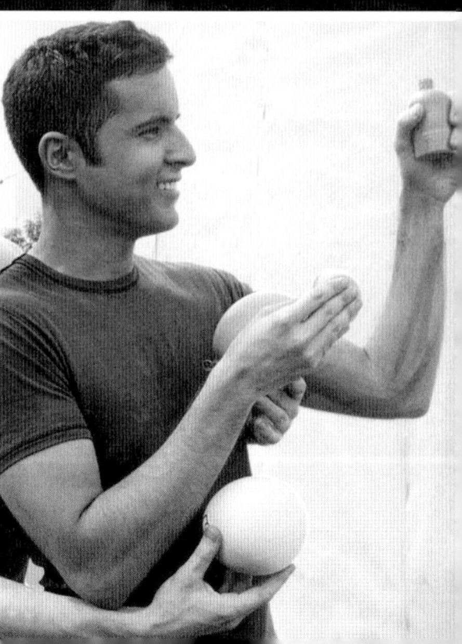

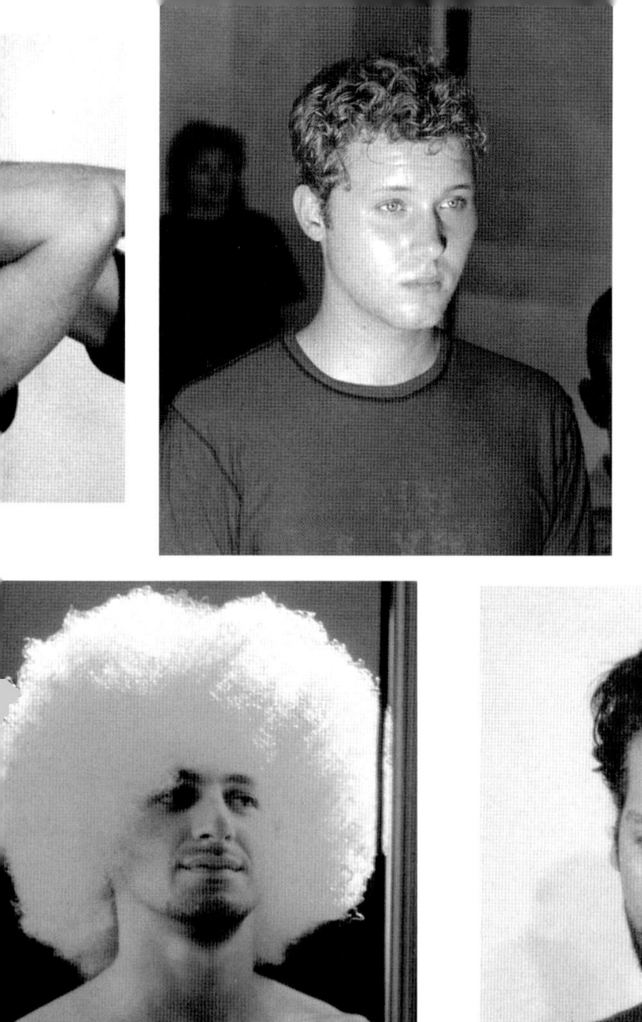
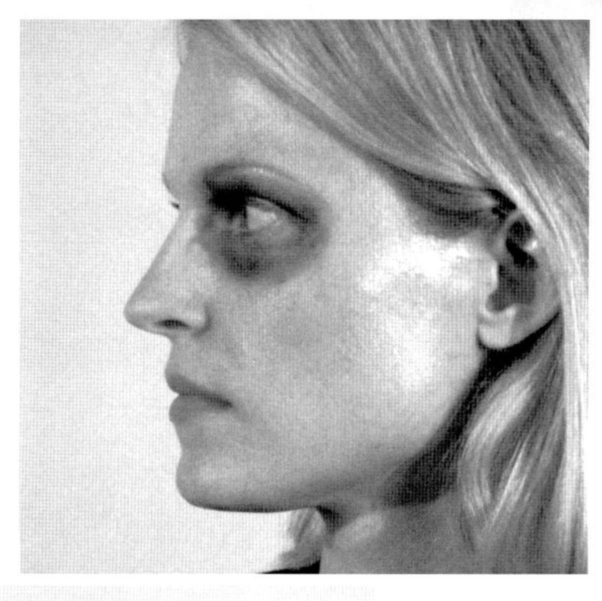
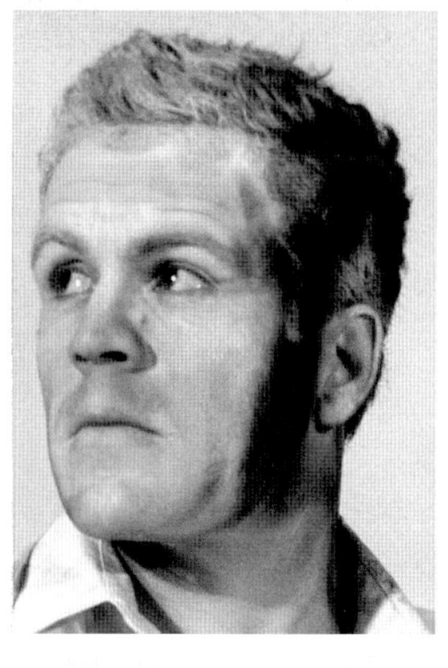
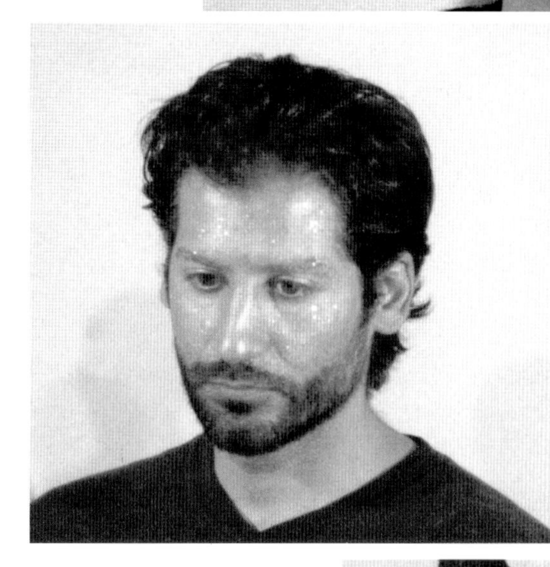
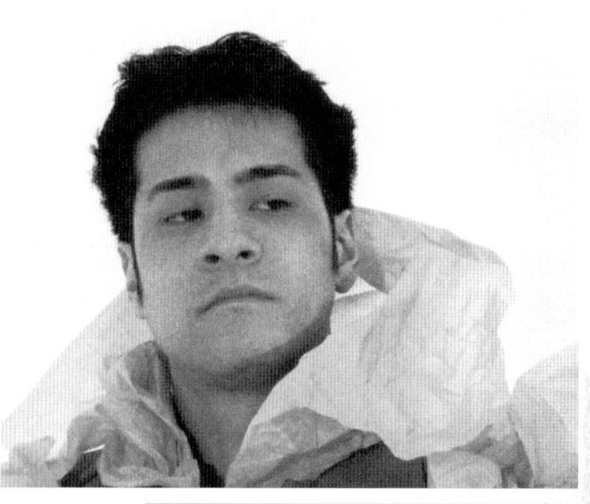
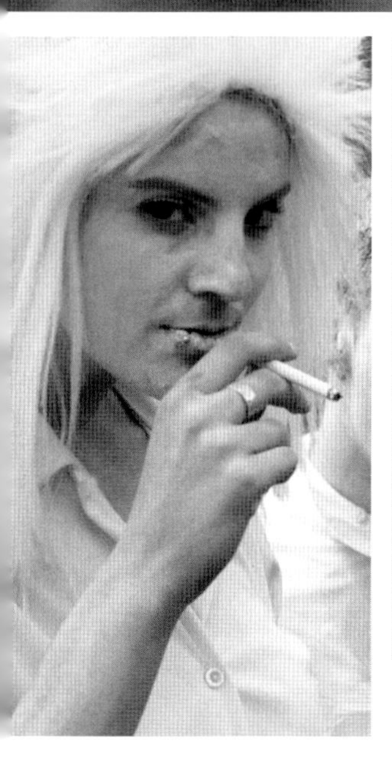
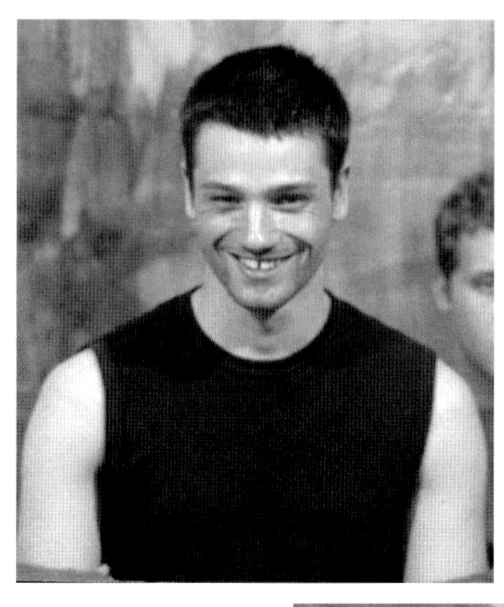
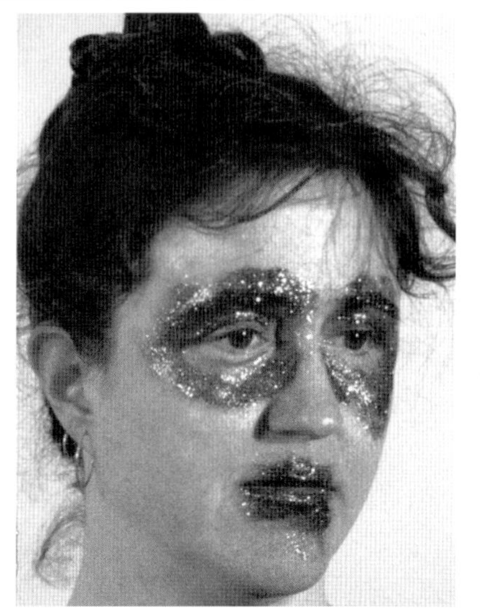
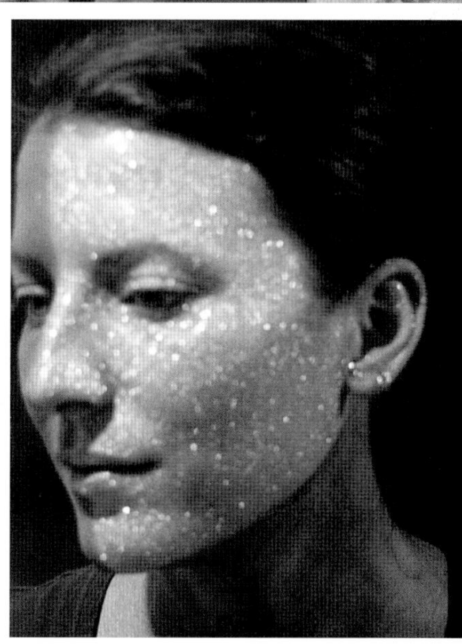
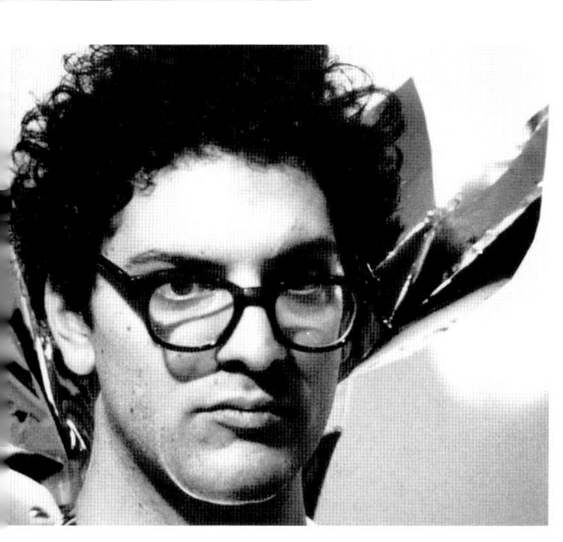
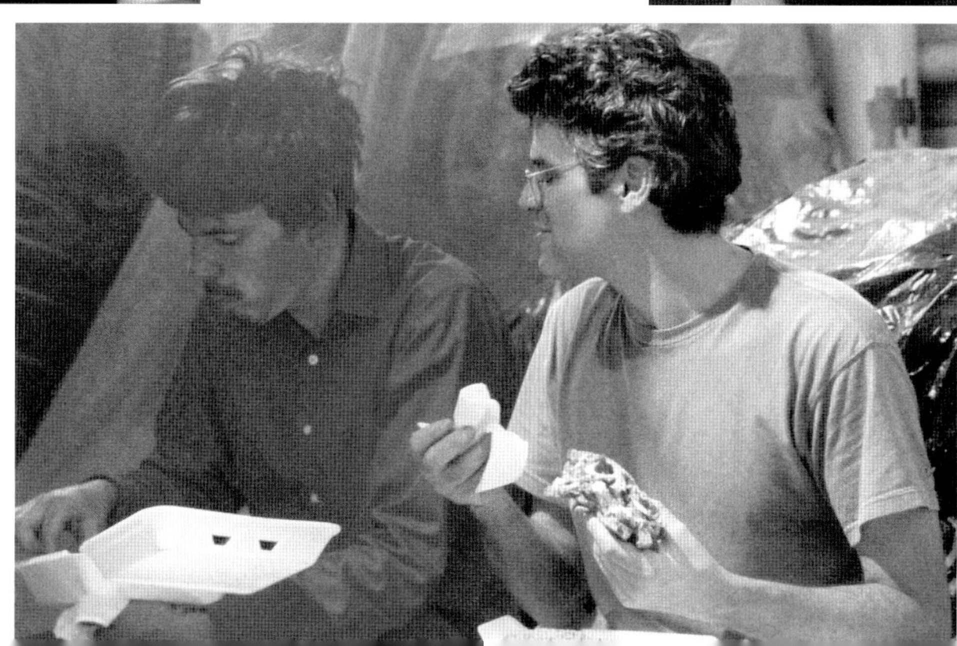

VIDEOGRAPHY

Videosketch #1, 1998. 59 seconds.
On camera: Oliver Herring; Off camera: Mitchell Marco; Editing: Oliver Herring and Luis Moreno

Videosketch #2, 1998. 46 seconds.
On camera: Oliver Herring; Off camera: Peter Krashes; Editing: Oliver Herring and Luis Moreno; Soundtrack: Oliver
Herring.

Videosketch #3, 1998. 1 minute, 3 seconds.
On camera: Oliver Herring; Off camera: Peter Krashes; Editing: Oliver Herring and Luis Moreno; Soundtrack: Oliver
Herring.

Videosketch #4, 1998. 1 minute, 13 seconds (looped).
On camera: Oliver Herring, Peter Krashes; Off camera: Mitchell Marco, Matthew Goodrich, Peter Krashes; Editing: Oliver
Herring and Luis Moreno; Soundtrack: Oliver Herring.

Exit – Videosketch #6, 1999. 8 minutes, 51 seconds, looped.
On camera: Oliver Herring, Miek Coccia, Matthew Goodrich, Caroline Duval-Arnould, Filip Noterdaeme Davide Borella
Off camera: Oliver Herring, Peter Krashes, Mitchell Marco, Matthew Goodrich, David Kalka; Editing: Oliver Herring and
David Dixon (The Outpost); Soundtrack: Oliver Herring

Two One-Day Sketches, 2000. 6 minutes, 52 seconds, looped. On camera: Fran Ferraro, Miek Coccia, Filip
Noterdaeme, Jennie Frost, Nancy Yousef, Oliver Herring; Off camera: Peter Krashes, Oliver Herring Editing: Oliver
Herring and David Dixon (The Outpost); Soundtrack: Oliver Herring

The Sum and Its Parts, 2000. 10 minutes, 35 seconds, looped. On camera: Miek Coccia; Off camera: Oliver Herring;
Editing: Oliver Herring and Richard Gordon (The Outpost) Soundtrack: Oliver Herring

Pure Sublimation, 2000–2001. 27 seconds, looped. On camera: Sasha Drvis, Mary Helen Harvey, Caroline
Duval- Arnould, Tracy, Miek Coccia, Fran Ferraro, Joyce Pensato, Luis Moreno, Filip Noterdaeme, Matthew Goodrich,
Davis Thompson-Moss, and five kids who joined us towards the evening; Off Camera: Oliver Herring,
Peter Krashes, David Kalka, David Dixon, Richard Gordon; Editing: Oliver Herring and David Dixon (The Outpost);
Soundtrack: Oliver Herring

Sketch for Little Dances of Misfortunes, 2001. 1 minute, 40 seconds. On camera: Miek Coccia; Off camera: Oliver
Herring; Editing: Oliver Herring and David Dixon (The Outpost); Soundtrack: Johan Baptist Krumpholz

Little Dances of Misfortunes, 2001. On camera: Miek Coccia, Caroline Duval-Arnould, Mary-Helen Harvey,
Joyce Pensato, Javier Piñòn; Off camera: Oliver Herring, Peter Krashes

Videosketch #5, 2001. On camera: Oliver Herring Off camera: Peter Krashes; Editing: Oliver Herring and David Dixon
(The Outpost); Soundtrack: Oliver Herring

Sleepless Nights, 2001. On camera: Cecilia Dean, Cheryl Horsfall, Miek Coccia, David Kalka, Starr Figura,
Javier Piñòn, Elizabeth Kley, Joyce Pensato, Jeffrey Sperber, Davis Thompson-Moss, Brandon Greenbaum, Chris
Dorland, Luis Moreno, Oliver Herring; Off camera: Oliver Herring, Peter Krashes Editing: Oliver Herring
and David Dixon (The Outpost); Soundtrack: Oliver Herring

Acknowledgements

This is an artist book and I was told I don't have to thank anybody, but I really should. First of all, Iwant to thank Kristin Chambers, curator of the Cleveland Center for Contemporary Art, for this wonderful opportunity as well as for her enthusiasm, guidance, and lots of patience. It has been an immense pleasure to work with her. I would like to thank Jill Snyder, Director of the CCCA and the Board of Trustees for embracing and supporting my project. I am grateful to Toby Devan Lewis, without whose generous support the exhibition and publication would not have been possible. Thanks to the entire staff of the CCCA for helping to realize the exhibition, especially Amy Gilman, Ginger Spivey, and Ray Juaire. I want to thoroughly thank all the people who worked to make this beautiful book: Peter Krashes, Matthew Goodrich, David Lowe, and Beverly Joel. Your suggestions, know-how, and calm under pressure were greatly appreciated.

I want to express particular thanks to Max Protetch, who has always given me carte blanche to do what I want and supported it, or even better — tried to support it. Thanks to Josie Browne, director at Max Protetch Gallery, whose love for art and ability to communicate that love are always inspiring. Unfortunately for her, these are not the only virtues that I rely on her for. My thanks to the entire staff at Max Protetch Gallery for their efforts on my behalf.

Thanks to all the collaborators who have enriched my work. In particular Mitchell Marco and Dafna Shalom, who helped in the studio when much of the work in this book was made. Both of them are excellent artists. A special thanks to the participants of my videos: Miek Coccia, who has been in almost all of my videos and without whom 'The Sum of It's Parts' would not have been made, Davide Borella, Cecilia Dean, Christopher Dorland, Sascha Drvis, Caroline Duval-Arnould, Fran Ferraro, Starr Figura, Jennie Frost, Matthew Goodrich, Brandon Greenbaum, Mary-Helen Harvey, Cheryl Horsfall, David Kalka, Elizabeth Kley, Peter Krashes, Mitchell Marco, Luis Moreno, Filip Noterdaeme, Javier Pinon, Joyce Pensato, Brian Reedy, Jeffrey Sperber, David Thompson-Moss, Tracy, and Nancy Yousef. Thank you for your inspiration, input, humor, friendship and for your valuable time. Also thanks to David Dixon of The Outpost, Richard Gordon, and Luis Moreno for helping to edit my videos.

Thanks to my parents, Marianne and Hugh who understand when I am really busy.

It is difficult to fully express my gratitude to Peter Krashes, whose hands and thoughts and talent and patience and sacrifice are everywhere in this book, the exhibition, my work and my life.

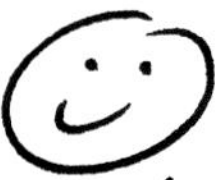

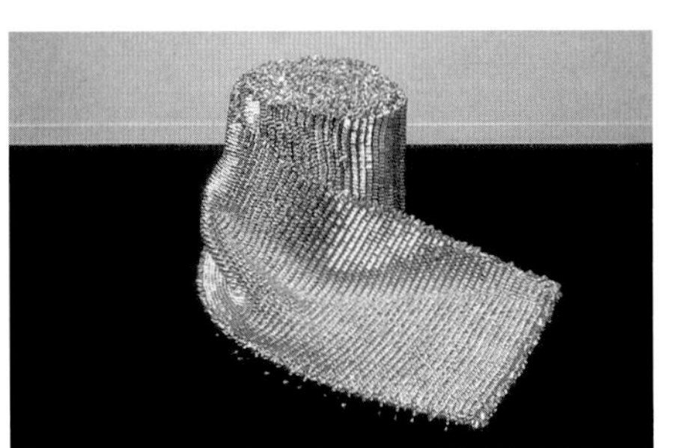